CW00555602

WHERE DOES GOD GO ON MONDAY?

DANNY GUGLIELMUCCI

NEW WINE PRESS

New Wine Ministries
PO Box 17
Chichester
West Sussex
United Kingdom
PO19 2AW

Copyright © 2008 Danny Guglielmucci

All rights reserved. No part of this publication may be reproduced, stored
in a retrieval system, or transmitted in any form or by any means, electronic,
mechanical, photocopying or otherwise, without the prior written consent of
the publisher. Short extracts may be used for review purposes.

Scripture quotations are taken from the Holy Bible, New Living Translation
copyright © 1996, 2004 by Tyndale Charitable Trust. Used by permission of
Tyndale House Publishers.

NKJV – New King James Version. Copyright © 1982 by Thomas Nelson, Inc.

ISBN 978-1-903725-96-2

Typeset by CRB Associates, Reepham, Norfolk
Cover design by Daniel Chattaway, www.edgechurch.com
Printed in Australia

CONTENTS

Foreword   7

PART ONE:
REPOSITIONING THE CHURCH

Chapter 1 **Let's Try Something New**   11
Where Are All the Workers?   15
How Did We Get Here?   19

Chapter 2 **Getting the Salt Out of the Shaker**   25
What Is God Saying?   26
Who Is God Sending?   35
What Will Be the Result?   39
Growing in Influence   42

PART TWO:
SUNDAY-MONDAY CHURCH

Chapter 3 **Sunday and Monday Church Working Together**   47
Seeing the Bigger Picture   52
Not "Either/Or" but "Both"   54
Who Builds Monday Church?   57

Chapter 4 **How We Began to Build Monday Church**   63
Paying the Price of Change   71
Expressions of Monday Church   72

Chapter 5 **Our Journey – Your Journey?**   81
The Spirit of Elijah   86

PART THREE:
CHANGING YOUR CHURCH CULTURE

Chapter 6 **Come, Let Us Reason Together**   93
What Kind of Church Do We Need
     to Become?   98
Changing the Atmosphere of Your Church   100

About the Author   107

Contact Information   109

FOREWORD

For the many years that I have been travelling, I have seen a common thread among the churches that are thriving and having an impact in their community. They love God and understand that God did not save them so they could form a believer's club, but He saved, called, and equipped them to reach out and love people. I'm amazed at how many believers today get saved and then essentially become a recluse within the church, never wanting to touch the "unclean" lest they get what they have.

Our churches are to be beacons of light; places of refuge that people come to be encouraged and strengthened on Sunday in order to impact their spheres of influence on Monday. We get in trouble when we consider our churches to be a club and you have to be saved in order to be in the club. Is this the example that Jesus lived? Of course not! He hung out and ate meals with prostitutes and sinners, even the mafia of the day! He opened His heart to all who needed a helping hand. And guess who Jesus railed against? Those religious people who had become focused on the fact you had to be "in the club" before you could be helped in any way.

We all have a sphere of influence in our lives that God has called us to and during our time on earth we possess that power to instil change. That may be in giving to an organization that helps orphans around the world, or it may be helping the person in the next office who is having marital problems, or it could be buying a meal for a homeless person down the street. When we have a heart of compassion in us, God will open our eyes to all the situations that are around us each day that we can speak life into and bring wholeness to.

I'm always interested in books written by people who are living the message in their own lives and I can honestly say, by being with Pastor Danny, that this is a message that transformed his life, spread to his church, and is now going throughout the world. The message in this book was written out of years of experience, trials, failures and successes. You can be rest assured that *Where Does God Go on Monday?* is not a book with hypothetical concepts; it will challenge you to live the life God has called you to.

Pastor Danny is a great personal friend and a man of God whose desire is to help people grow into what God has called them to. I believe that if you open your heart to hear what the Holy Spirit will say to you through this book, you can expect your life to forever be changed.

John Bevere
Author and Speaker
Messenger International
Colorado Springs, Australia and United Kingdom

PART ONE

REPOSITIONING THE CHURCH

CHAPTER 1

LET'S TRY SOMETHING NEW

Growing up in a pastor's home and spending most of my life in and around the Church, my worldview for a long time was shaped by Christian convictions that weren't always "Christian" convictions. I'm a little embarrassed to say that it took me so many years to realize that the Bible wasn't just a book for Christians or about what takes place within the walls of what we call "church". Lately I have begun to see so clearly that God's Word, our roadmap to life, is not just concerned with church-life, what happens in our churches each Sunday, but it's more about Monday-through-Sunday-life — what happens when the life of the church spills out into society. After twenty-four years of ministry I have come to this

11

conclusion: great sermons alone will never change the world! We need to try something new.

But this is not a book recommending some new technique or model for church growth. This is a book that calls us to get back to basics; a book that says, actually, the answer has been plain to see in the Word of God all along, if only we would see it.

> **"The day is upon us where we can no longer afford to hear fantastic, inspirational messages in our church services on Sunday that somehow fail to make their way into our workplaces, homes and families."**

I'm reminded of a story I heard of a pastor who stood before his people and delivered the same message week after week. Eventually, when questioned by some of his team as to why he was doing this, the reply came, "The power is not in the message alone but in the application of its truth. Perhaps when we begin to activate this sermon we can move on to the next?"

The point of the story is to illustrate how eager the Church is to move on to the "next big thing". We love new techniques, new methods and think that these will solve our problems. But our "problem" is that we never really grasp or apply the truth of what already lies before us. We can sit in church week after week and hear sermon after sermon and somehow still miss it. James, in his letter to the Church, points out that we need to grow up to the place where we are no longer only hearers of the Word, but doers – people who have the truth of the Bible active in our daily lives. The day is upon us where we can no longer afford to hear fantastic, inspirational messages in our church services on Sunday that somehow fail to make their way into our workplaces, homes and families. Where does God go after church? Is He not interested in helping us become better people, stronger families and better leaders? We all need to ask ourselves the most important question: "Where is the power of the message of Jesus in my life?"

So much of what the Church of the twenty-first century has become is characterised by an "event" mentality towards our faith. For many it has become a weekly visit with Jesus for our regular pick-me-up before returning to the reality of our daily struggle – and these two aspects of life seem to have very little to do with one another. Too many are living powerless, ineffective and largely unfulfilling "Christian" lives. Yet the Jesus we read about in the Bible, the Jesus we preach from our platforms on Sunday, He was something else, something more. He was interested in people's lives, their loves and losses. He wept with them, healed them and ate in their homes. Very little of Jesus' ministry actually occurred within the walls of the "Church".

It is my deepest desire to see people becoming like Jesus; to live life how He lived it. I want to see people get hold of a significant, purpose-filled life, empowered by encounter and equipped with revelation; for them to wake up on a Monday morning knowing that God hasn't "left the building" and He is not waiting for them at church. He is right there with them and church can happen for them today, on Monday. Whatever lies ahead of them on Monday they will be building something of significance, building the kingdom of God in the most unlikely places.

No one begins their Christian journey with the goal of living two lives divided between weekends and weekdays. That would be crazy. But anyone who has been around for longer than five minutes will know that things rarely turn out the way we plan them. As we walk this journey of faith we have to admit that often we find ourselves operating at a level far below where we know we should be. But what if things could be different? What if we could live an undivided life – a life where we lived in the moment, where every day was "Sunday" and every opportunity a God opportunity? In other words, church would no longer be something we attended, but church would happen wherever we were and whatever we were doing. In fact, our work would become church!

It can happen. In fact, I have come to realize that the Bible insists this is the "normal" Christian life. If we will just allow God to impact our lives in a deeper way than having fuzzy feelings on a Sunday, if we will allow our relationship with Him to be more than a weekend routine, then our lives will change dramatically. We will no longer merely work for a living, but we will understand that we work for Jesus and our work life will become a kingdom adventure! God's ideal for us is that earning a living is just a by-product of living for Christ. Instead of "holding down a job", our focus should be on working as an agent in God's kingdom, promoting His cause and pursuing His purposes.

The Bible clearly shows that Jesus lived this holistic, integrated approach to life and there was no gap between His work-life/home-life. He just lived one life before God! He didn't spend His time trying to herd people into church so that they could hear His sermons and get saved. He made no separation between His behaviour in the Church and on the street. In fact He battled against the mindset that says such a distinction exists throughout His entire ministry life. Jesus went out among the people – especially those who were the most needy – and He met them where they were, touching them and changing lives.

These days, being invited along to church, however great it may be, is not a very attractive prospect to most people – especially in a post-modern society. But when people see the Church not as an institution, but as real people wanting to connect with them, free of any agenda other than to be the hands and feet of Jesus so that the kingdom of God touches their lives in a powerful way, it has an altogether different impact. We read in Matthew 9:35 that,

"Jesus travelled through all the towns and villages of that area, teaching in the synagogues and announcing the Good News about the Kingdom. And he healed every kind of disease and illness."

Notice it does not say that Jesus went around announcing the Good News about "the Church" but about "the kingdom". He didn't hand out invitations to come to the Synagogue for the next event, He just reached out and met people's needs. Jesus knew that what people needed was not an invitation to an event, but a touch from God that would change their lives. He felt a great compassion for the crowds of people who constantly swarmed around Him, immersed in their problems, looking for answers. He described them as being like "sheep without a shepherd" and He reached out to them. His message was about a Gospel that empowers you to live life. This same message encourages us to build a church without walls.

Where Are All the Workers?

On this same occasion Jesus commented to His disciples that,

"The harvest is great, but the workers are few. So pray to the Lord who is in charge of the harvest; ask him to send more workers into his fields."

(MATTHEW 9:37–38)

I often used to wonder, "Why is it that God is so short of workers when there are so many Christian people crying out week after week for an opportunity for God to use them?"

Suddenly it occurred to me: "The reason there are so few workers in the field is because all the workers are in the Church." The more I thought about it the more I realized the truth of it! There are so few workers actually doing the work of the kingdom because the majority of us are busy trying to build church from the inside out. We have given so much attention to the mechanics of Sunday church that somehow our real mission on earth has become sidetracked.

> **"The time is coming, and indeed has already arrived, when God will take His Church on a journey into completely new territory."**

Our continual focus on Sunday church has helped us to become ever more introspective and self-obsessed. This in turn has created an epidemic in our churches where we are so focused on our own needs that we linger in the church when we really should be out in the fields doing God's work. It seems to me that if, after several years of being saved and belonging to a church, a Christian is still struggling to live a life where their beliefs and convictions affect the way they do life, then we, the Church, are really doing something wrong. Surely after being saved and in a church for any decent period of time there should be an awareness of a purpose that goes beyond just the guarantee of an eternity with Jesus? If we can't build a church where this is a reality is it any wonder that the corporate Church is seen as a weak institution without the power to change a life, much less a community or the world?

Don't get me wrong, I love the Church and believe with all my heart that it is God's chosen instrument for reaching mankind and evangelising the earth. But I am convinced that we have created a church culture that is too comfortable and largely un-challenging. We have turned church into a kind of spiritual social club where many inward-looking programs help establish and maintain a cozy comfort zone. Believers are content to be spoon fed teaching that enhances their own spiritual life, but are rarely if ever encouraged to look beyond themselves to the needs of others.

I don't believe we can allow such a culture to continue. The time is coming, and indeed has already arrived, when God will take His Church on a journey into completely new territory. Change can be really difficult, but some Christians will come easily, ready to embrace the challenge. Others, who have "enjoyed" the comfort of a less challenging existence, will come dragging their feet. But one thing is for sure: we are all going on this journey because Jesus has promised: *"I will build my Church and the gates of hell shall not prevail against it"* (Matthew 16:18). The Church that Jesus is building is the *only* plan, there is no "Plan B". The Church is His only and most potent plan to bring about lasting change and transformation. It won't happen through the agencies of government or politics or by the leadership of inspirational public leaders, despite their best intentions, but through the Church of Jesus Christ. God intends to use us powerfully to accomplish His purposes.

A pastor friend of mine wrote,

"There is a growing awareness that we cannot continue to do the same old things and expect a different result. If we want to be the salt and light we as the Church were created to be, we have to do something different, we have to *be* something different. Community transformation is not found in programs, strategies, campaigns or tactics. For most of us it will take nothing less than a shift of seismic proportions in what the Church has to be in the third millennium."

The Church will truly become an effective force in the earth when we focus on demonstrating the kingdom to others instead of just talking about it. Jesus asserted this view in Matthew 5:13–16 when He said,

> *"You are the salt of the earth. But what good is salt if it has lost its flavour? Can you make it salty again? It will be thrown out and trampled underfoot as worthless. You are the light of the world – like a city on a hilltop that cannot be hidden. No one lights a lamp and then puts it under a basket. Instead, a lamp is placed on a stand, where it gives light to everyone in the house. In the same way, let your good deeds shine out for all to see, so that everyone will praise your heavenly Father."*

In other words, there is only one way that people who do not know God will ever encounter Him in a genuine and real way: when they see our good deeds and when they see the kingdom of God invading their everyday lives. In fact, the Bible actually says that as we demonstrate the goodness of God it is possible for people to come to a realization of who He is without ever setting foot inside the four walls of the Church (1 Peter 2:12). What an incredible thought! Over the last couple of years God has challenged our church to do precisely that – to look outwards and to concentrate on touching the lives of others with the goodness of God. I am so grateful to the members of our church for the way they have all embraced what God has begun in us and for the favour we have found with our community as we have made the decision to be the hands and feet of Jesus outside of the church. As a result we have begun to see our community transformed.

We have heard story after story of people being impacted by receiving unexpected food parcels, by church members being there for them in their time of grief, by someone helping them in their time of need. Since we shifted our focus outward instead of inward we have received literally hundreds of "thank you" letters from people whose lives have been touched by the kingdom. When I read them I think, "Yes, *this* is the Church!" This is what I imagine Jesus doing if He was in my shoes. Our church is filled with people who are consumed with a passion to live a life larger than just their immediate needs. This book is certainly not to tell the world how great we are, but simply to pass on the power of what we have learnt in living "Monday church" and the transformation it can bring, not only to our churches, but more importantly our communities.

How Did We Get Here?

The Church has seen periods of incredible influence throughout history. It has shaped public morality, founded hospitals, educational facilities, entire legal systems and social welfare organisations. It was designed to be an unbelievably powerful force in the earth. I believe it will be again, despite over the last few centuries, particularly in the West, seeing serious decline in many areas.

Less than 300 years after the birth of Christ, the Church had shown such tremendous strength and growth that it was thought the entire civilised world could be evangelised by AD 500. The theologian and historian Turtullian[1] wrote in AD 212:

> "We have filled your cities, islands, fortified towns, country towns, camps, tribes, palaces and governments. Almost all the citizens you have in your cities are now Christian."

1. Turtullian (AD 160–225). The first theologian to use the word "Trinity" and who wrote against the persecution of Christians.

In the year AD 180, Theophilus, an elder of the church at Antioch, wrote, "The whole world is now filled with Christian inhabitants."

In AD 251 a letter from Cornelius of Rome to Fabius of Antioch informed him that in the church of Rome there were more than 140 ministries supported full time by the church and that they also supported more than 1,500 widows and orphans.

I remember reading a study entitled "The number of Christians at the beginning of the 4th Century", which stated that between 7.5 and 15 million people were Christians at the height of that period.

But something clearly went wrong to get us to where we are today. Something caused the downward spiral that the Western Church is battling to reverse while the Church in other parts of the world is flourishing. Without wishing to oversimplify things I believe three main factors led to the loss of power that our part of the Body of Christ has suffered from. I think it is helpful for us to think about these factors as we engage with God afresh and seek His heart for the future of our churches.

The Church lost its distinctiveness

There is no doubt that the Church lost some of its "saltiness" through times of heavy persecution, but it has also suffered, I believe, from generations who, in an effort to make the message of the Gospel contemporary, relevant and palatable to the masses have watered down the Bible's teaching on righteousness. They have also undermined the divine nature of the person of Jesus Christ and have questioned the truth and accuracy of the Word of God itself.

The Church has lost much of its power because it has not been clear or united in its message. But we cannot afford to be a Church that preaches anything less than the fullness of who

God is. We cannot take the Word of God and try to make it more "acceptable" to a broken world, because by diluting it we undermine its truth. We cannot suggest that Jesus was a great man but not really the Son of God or that the resurrection didn't really happen. If we do the Church will be powerless because this is the heart, the very essence of our message. All of who we are and what we are called to be and to do is tied to all that Jesus is. If we cease to represent the truth about Jesus then we will cease to be a force for good and to have any positive influence on our community. We will simply be an institution that is irrelevant and ineffective – a monument to the past.

> "The Church has lost much of its power because it has not been clear or united in its message. But we cannot afford to be a Church that preaches anything less than the fullness of who God is."

If the Church is to regain its influence in our world we must once again commit ourselves to preaching righteousness, the truth of the Word of God. The Church cannot remain a movement that is a monument to something God was doing in the past. It has to be a movement that is irresistible and irreversible back to the truth. We need the Bible more than ever and we need to remain true to the person of Jesus Christ. Our job as His representatives is to love every sinner, love every person who is trapped and desperate, and stand up for the truth. In many other parts of the world today people are coming to a saving knowledge of Jesus and are being transformed and renewed by His power, but if we lose our ability to teach the truth about Jesus then we might as well give up. We'll be just another social club with great intentions and fall far short of our potential.

The division between clergy and laity

Another challenge arose for the Church when we drew a line between what we perceived to be the "congregation" and the "priesthood" or "leadership". Gradually our leaders have been separated out from among the people who attend our churches and turned into professional preachers. The "ministry" has moved away from being a recognition of calling and anointing and it has become a career. Studies have proven over and over again that effective church growth is best achieved through personal evangelism, but we have somehow taken that task away from ordinary people and put it into the hands of "professional" evangelists. The clergy/laity divide has created a mentality in the average churchgoer to expect meetings to be driven from the platform. We have allowed our Christianity to be lowered to the point where we are motivated by events rather than by the divine purpose we were created for. Church members have become spectators instead of active participants, an audience rather than part of the family. As soon as that shift began to take place the Church began to lose power.

The truth is, every single Christian is anointed to be a minister of Jesus Christ and the sooner we begin to operate with this mindset the sooner we will see the Church we dream of and pray for. We are all brothers and sisters in the Body of Christ. Just because some have been given the title "Pastor" or "Evangelist" should not prevent others from functioning in these roles. And those with the titles "Pastor" or "Evangelist" should not feel undermined when others lead more people to Christ than they do! If God puts a great dream in someone's heart and uses them mightily for His purposes, fantastic! Far be it for us to feel threatened or insecure. We are all in this together and we need to celebrate whenever broken lives are touched, rather than arguing over titles and positions.

The introduction of church buildings

From the time that Alexander Severus built the first church building the Church has been burdened with a preoccupation with buildings. Buildings have become the focal point and have distracted from the church's main purposes of worship, teaching, evangelism and breaking bread together in the community. What once used to take place in the heart of the community in houses and small gatherings has been uprooted and moved behind the walls of specially constructed church buildings. What started with good intentions to build places for Christians to meet together and worship has actually contributed towards Christians substituting "being the church" for "going to church". Over time this has caused believers to lose sight of the fundamental purpose of church and to become introverted in their faith. Today, a great percentage of believers struggle to share their faith and many have never personally led anybody to Jesus Christ. The average church spends the vast majority of its time and money on the already-converted. All of this has created a trend towards a type of consumer Christianity which rarely satisfies.

> **"The starting point for change must be with you and me as we begin to grasp what is on God's heart and decide that the status quo is no longer good enough..."**

I'm not arguing against having church buildings, but stressing that we need to recapture the purpose of them. We have to actively and deliberately strategise against our buildings becoming an end in themselves. If God has given us buildings and property, it is for a reason, and that reason is to be a beacon of light to our community. We have an opportunity to use our church buildings in ways that help break down the mindsets and old stereotypes among the community regarding what church could or should look like. Just recently some members of local government visited our church and among the many positive comments they made one of them remarked, "Wow! You guys do things well." I believe in excellence and in showing people that only the best will do for God, but there must be a balance. The balance is: "What's the point of having a great looking salt shaker if the salt always stays inside it and never gets used?"

I believe these factors have contributed to where we are now. But we cannot allow any of these things to hold back the Church of the present/future. The starting point for change must be with you and me as we begin to grasp what is on God's heart and decide that the status quo is no longer good enough and that we have a role to play in changing the future.

If we accept these reasons for the downward spiral, and really the evidence is compelling, what steps can we take to begin to reverse the trend? Surely we must find ways of envisioning and empowering the people once again to *be* the Church – to be all that God intended them to be and to do all that He has for them to do.

We must get the salt out of the shaker!

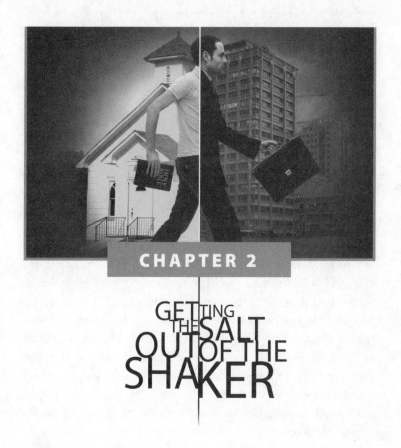

CHAPTER 2

GETTING THE SALT OUT OF THE SHAKER

If we can accept that the twenty-first-century Church is faced with some very real challenges due, at least in part, to the three factors mentioned at the end of the last chapter, we need to know what God has to say about it and what will help us get back on track. I believe that God is saying a number of things to us, confirmed by what others are saying or beginning to say around the world, that will help us to get back on track. If we are willing to hear God's heart on these issues it will turn around the Church as we know it and help us to once again become the influential force we were designed to be. In this chapter I want to ask and answer three questions:

- What is God saying?
- Who is God sending?
- What will be the result?

WHAT IS GOD SAYING?

We need to be more "out" than "in"

First and foremost I believe God is saying to His Church, "Get the salt out of the shaker!" God is not calling us to attend any more conferences on church growth or learn any more evangelism techniques, though such things are great when married to purpose. He is calling us to engage our communities like never before and allow the genuine nature of who we are to bring the transformation. Church life needs to shift to being more about "out" than "in". If we could take that one simple phrase on board, work through all its implications, and live it out loud, we would begin to see a huge shift, not only in our church culture but in how we are perceived by those we are called to reach.

We need to be thinking "out" and not "in" when we sit down and plan our annual church programs. If we do it will revolutionise the impact our churches have on our communities in a very short space of time. In church we are supposed to get equipped by teaching, preaching and discipleship programs, but whose lives are we actually changing if we leave it there? All we are doing is helping already-saved Christians to fill up on all this teaching and equipping, but we're not encouraging them to exercise what they already have. The world we are called to reach cares little about our great teaching and discipleship! Their message to the Church is, "Tell us how much you care before you tell us how much you know" or better still, "Show us how much you care before you even open your mouth!" All people really want to know is whether God's love is real and tangible for them, and whether anybody cares with no strings attached.

> **"Church life needs to shift to being more about 'out' than 'in'. If we could take that one simple phrase on board, work through all its implications, and live it out loud, we would begin to see a huge shift, not only in our church culture but in how we are perceived by those we are called to reach."**

All over the world God is speaking to His people about connecting the church with their local community. What is happening in our church in Adelaide is happening everywhere. Globally God is encouraging His people to get the "salt out of the shaker" and to live out their faith in the midst of their communities. We must get the balance right because God wants His Church back!

We need to get back to basics with our ministry gifts

I believe God is also calling us to stop relying so completely on the fivefold ministry gifts listed in Ephesians 4:11. We have talked about the problems the Church has had because of the clergy/laity divide. We now have to be careful that we don't use the presence of these God-given gifts as an excuse not to do the work of God ourselves. It is far too easy to depend on those specially gifted by God to build the Church, assuming that it is their responsibility to do *all* of the work. This is such a wrong understanding of the purpose of these gifts to the Body. Their purpose is to train and equip other believers so that *they* can do the work of the ministry! It was never God's purpose that they should be anything other than equippers and facilitators. Their calling is to mobilize the Body of Christ at large to *be* the Church.

It seems especially common for people to think that witnessing and sharing the Gospel is best done by those gifted as Evangelists. Nothing could be further from the truth! Every one of us has that responsibility as Matthew 9:37–38 makes clear. The job of the Ephesians 4 Evangelist is to train us all how to be better witnesses and how to share the Gospel more effectively. But this common error just illustrates how comfortable we have become with the idea that "ministry" is what paid church staff do. And the upshot of this mentality is that people then get upset when the church isn't run the way they would like it.

People get upset when, for instance, the senior pastor sends out one of his pastoral team to visit them instead of visiting them himself. I have even heard instances of people leaving churches because, they say, "The pastor never visited me!" Apparently, no other pastor was good enough – it had to be the senior minister. But the senior pastor's job is to train and equip others to do the work of the ministry. There are also those who will look at who is due to preach at church next week and decide to give it a miss if it's not the senior minister – as if no one else in the church is good enough to teach them something.

The truth is, if we are ever going to become the type of significant churches our communities need us to be, the "work" of the ministry must be something we all take care of. It cannot be left to the few. Such a fundamental mis-understanding of the purpose of the Ephesians 4 gifts has led to many a pastor becoming burnt out or having a nervous breakdown as they try to meet the demands of doing all the work themselves. How much more powerful is it when every one in the Body carries, burning within us, the burden and mantle of the call of God for our life. Then, instead of being run ragged, the fivefold ministry gifts can be released to function in their true capacity, training and releasing others to be active in God's kingdom.

> **"The truth is, if we are ever going to become the type of significant churches our communities need us to be, the 'work' of the ministry must be something we all take care of. It cannot be left to the few."**

I believe the Church has been bottlenecked for years because of misunderstanding on this one issue. Let's remember that the ministry gifts exist to equip the Body of Christ to go out and do miracles and ministry during the week – so that they can come back on Sunday ready to celebrate all that God has done in and through them and to be refuelled to go back to their mission field and do it all again!

In short, it's time to do *life*, not church!

We are not of the world, but we are in it

One of the key things God said to me during our own church's transition to becoming outward focused was: "You need to be insulated, not isolated." To me this suggested that God wants us to be very definitely *present* in the world, not cut off from it or divorced from reality, but not affected by its value systems either. The problem for the most part is that it is easier to be of the world but not in it; to behave in ways which are not so different and fool ourselves that because we separate ourselves by our outward behaviour, that somehow makes us godly. We need to avoid the two extremes of being (a) so spiritually minded we are of no earthly use, and (b) so worldly that we are no longer salt and light to those around us.

I get invited to a lot of functions and one thing that saddens me greatly is when I see Christians behaving no differently from the world we're endeavouring to change, and all in the name of "having a good time". Seeing Christians compromising and living so far below God's best for them is one of the most tragic things you will ever see. Like wearing a suit three sizes too big, it just doesn't fit! We don't have to copy what people do in the world in order to "fit in" and we can still absolutely be the life of the party without compromising. I have a goal whenever I go to a party that I'll have the noisiest table, the best fun and the most laughs. After all, didn't Jesus come so we could have life to the full? We just need to be like Jesus who was a friend of sinners and hung out with them all the time. Jesus was present with them, identified Himself with them, but He didn't have to be like them to prove Himself "acceptable".

We need to be like the tiny insect that scientists have discovered which can immerse itself in water without ever getting wet. Even when it plunges into deep water, the water never touches it because it is continually protected by a bubble of air that forms around it. Similarly, as Christians we need to be fully immersed in our culture but not infected by it – and not standing out like some religious crazy person either! We won't do ourselves or the world any favours by giving them the impression that we are strange or socially awkward misfits. Instead, Christians should be some of the most respected and admired people in our community, not for our own sake, but so that we represent Jesus well. Christians should be the most switched on people in our community, because we are insulated, but not isolated.

Some may ask, "Well, why do we need to be immersed in our environment? Aren't we called to be separate from the world?" Yes, we need to be separate from the world in the sense that we don't allow it's values and morality to become our values and morality. We have to retain our kingdom values. But we cannot afford to reach the place where its brokenness doesn't touch us, because then we will lose our compassion for the hurting and broken. We need to be touched yet untouched, because we have something inside of us that is greater than the world! Let's allow God to lead us out of our churches and into our communities – not to be contaminated, but to touch and transform others.

God is calling us to bless our communities, not bore them

I think I've lost count of the times someone has found out that I am a Christian and responded with, "Well, you don't look like one." What this suggests to me is that people have a mental picture of what the typical Christian looks like, and generally it's not a good one! People have developed the idea that Christians are boring, stuffy, prudish killjoys with poor social skills. How on earth did we earn that reputation? We should be known to be the most creative, colourful, interesting, diverse bunch of people on the planet. People should be fascinated and attracted by how different we are. It should draw them towards God, not turn them off Him. If we could move from a place of boring our communities with predictable rhetoric, always protesting and complaining about things, we may actually surprise them by blessing them just because we can. Maybe then they'd want our input.

It's quite amazing how God can take the most mundane things and turn them into opportunities for ministry if we'll just allow Him to. Being the hands and feet of Jesus to others could call for something as simple as making a cup of coffee for a workmate, helping someone to move house or stopping to help someone change a tyre. If we could just think outside the walls which confined us for so long, there are so many opportunities waiting for us. We can remove forever the image of Christianity as boring and show it to be a life filled with purpose and opportunity. How about dinner at my place?!

> "We are to take the kingdom of God into the marketplace and touch people's lives. We must build a Church without walls, a Church that is present in our communities Monday to Friday, twenty-four-seven."

It's time to proclaim the Good News

In Luke chapter 4 we read about the occasion, right at the beginning of His ministry, when Jesus was speaking at His local synagogue. Having been tempted by the devil in the wilderness He had returned, full of the power of the Spirit, to His childhood home in Nazareth. The verses He read, from Isaiah chapter 61, were carefully chosen because they were a statement of His credentials and His intent:

> " 'The Spirit of the Lord is upon me,
>   for he has anointed me to bring Good News to the poor.
> He has sent me to proclaim that captives will be released,
>   that the blind will see,
> that the oppressed will be set free,
>   and that the time of the Lord's favour has come.'
>
> He rolled up the scroll, handed it back to the attendant, and sat down. All eyes in the synagogue looked at him intently. Then he began to speak to them. 'The Scripture you've just heard has been fulfilled this very day!' "

(LUKE 4:18–21)

32

Effectively, Jesus was telling the people, "This is who I am, this is my mission, my ministry; these are the things that matter to Me." Just as the Spirit of the Lord was upon Jesus, He is upon us too, and we have the exact same ministry mandate on the earth as Jesus had – to see our communities transformed by the Good News. We are to take the kingdom of God into the marketplace and touch people's lives. We must build a Church without walls, a Church that is present in our communities Monday to Friday, twenty-four-seven. We need to listen to what God is saying to us and make a decision to shift our focus and therefore our priorities.

We need to raise up authentic Christianity

Have you ever thought about your church from the perspective of a person attending for the first time? God really challenged me recently to look with fresh eyes at all the things we do that would make absolutely no sense to our neighbours and friends. I really believe it's time that the Church began to get real and communicated with people in ways and with words they can understand.

If you were to take a non-English-speaking native Italian and drop them in the middle of Sydney they would have a fair amount of difficulty communicating with anyone. When you don't speak the language it can be very difficult to get your point across. In many ways the Church has become like an Italian in Sydney! We speak a language that few around us understand, have our own traditions quite different from those around us, and we may as well be from another country because we're not integrated into our community! When did you last hear someone on the street say, "Have you been washed in the blood of the Lamb?" The average un-churched person wouldn't have a clue what this phrase means. Why did Jesus talk so much about fishing and farming in His teaching and parables? Maybe it was because He understood who His audience was. I wonder if we have lost sight of our audience at times.

I realize that this is an extreme example, but the truth is we have grown isolated from the world we are called to reach. We need to begin to express the things of God in a language and in a way that people can understand without losing our reverence for who He is. We need to express ourselves in a way that shows people, "Jesus is real and He wants to be your friend." That's something anyone can understand.

It's important we learn how to do this with our worship, since it is such a central part of church life. In the Church some people have complained about modern worship saying that we need more theology in the lyrics of our songs. I don't know. Surely the greatest worship of all is that which comes from the heart of a life transformed, however it's expressed? A kid off the street who has wrestled with thoughts of suicide and struggled with the bondage of addiction is not likely to have a theological understanding of many of the things we would see as quite basic. Yet I think his/her revelation of the grace of God would be at least as powerful as our theology. Our church services should be a place of life where we make Jesus understood to our generation. If there is evidence that old hymns can touch a young generation, then let's keep singing them. If they are irrelevant, then let's sing something that reaches people. Let's have a style of service that causes complete unbelievers off the street to walk in and say, "Wow, these people are talking my language. This is a church I could belong to." I am not into music for music's sake. For me it's not about style (or volume for that matter). We have just got to get past personal preference and see what works. I believe God can anoint the music and the language of today, just as He did the music and language of the past.

It's time for the Church to regain its flavour! Genuine, authentic Christianity means that we should be the salt of the earth. That's why it's so sad when people say that Christians are hypocrites and worse than non-Christians. What a terrible indictment on the Church and a poor reflection on us. As Christians we are "on duty" twenty-four-seven. Our Christianity can no longer be a hat we take off and put on. We are called to live the life of a follower of Jesus, not just at weekends, but day in and day out – as modelled for us by the priests mentioned in 2 Chronicles 5:11:

> *"All the priests who were present had purified themselves, whether or not they were on duty that day."*

We have got to be real and live out our lives in our community with a level of authenticity not seen since the early Church. We are ambassadors of Christ. Every time we get annoyed with our neighbour, lose our cool over some issue, or go off the deep end, it puts another nail in the coffin for those who have no time for phoney Christians. Instead, week by week we should be growing into the image of Jesus Christ, becoming more like Him every day. If we had an anger problem five years ago, what are we doing to overcome it? How is the power of what we preach actively bringing change? Authentic Christianity means that we cooperate with God's process of sanctification. We may be saved immediately we give our lives to Christ, but our mind and our emotions need renewal on a daily basis. This is the journey we have signed up to and we need to press on in order to see transformation taking place.

WHO IS GOD SENDING?

This is an extract from an article I came across:

> "It is God who gave some to be pastors and teachers, to prepare God's people for works of service according

to Ephesians 4:11–12. In the typical church lay-people are asked to serve in five or six capacities: teach at Sunday school, work in the nursery, lead a home Bible study or a small group, sing in the choir, be an usher or a greeter, serve on a board or committee. Little wonder pastors lament that only 20% of their members are active. Could it be that the service opportunities are not broad enough to engage the energies and passions of the people in the church?

Robert Lewis knows that when people enter his church they are excited for about 4–5 years. How could they not be excited: fellowship, Bible, and Robert is an incredible teacher. But he observes that after around 5 years, people get bored with church if they are not involved with ministering to others. It was not until the church began to serve their community that members found their calling and now they are continuing to grow."

For a long time I have sought to preach from Scripture a message that encourages people to find their place in the Body of Christ and live out their calling. I have encouraged people to realize what gifts God has given them and use them. I thank God for the seven powerful, motivational gifts mentioned in Romans 12:6–8: prophecy, faith, teaching, giving, leadership, mercy and encouragement. These are all gifts that should be active in a healthy, properly functioning community of believers. However, for such a long time we have only interpreted these gifts in the context of Sunday church. We need to come to the realization that they don't exist simply to be used in the context of the four walls of our church services, but also to love and minister to the broken communities God has positioned us in. We cannot afford to get caught up in "ministry" for its own sake so that we lose our outward focus. We must do everything we do empowered for our purpose.

Each of us has a responsibility to find our place in the Body of Christ, the place in which God has designed us to function, where we will be at our most effective. For one person that may be teaching in children's ministry, but for another it might be working in an office, being salt and light amongst their un-churched colleagues. Neither person should feel guilty that they are not doing what the other person is doing. Each person should function in their own gift and calling, doing what God wants them to do.

> **"Each of us has a responsibility to find our place in the Body of Christ, the place in which God has designed us to function, where we will be at our most effective. For one person that may be teaching in children's ministry, but for another it might be working in an office, being salt and light amongst their un-churched colleagues."**

Your calling might not be to serve God as a home group leader, but to serve God in the business world and do something for Him in that arena that is powerful and life transforming. Our job, as the church, is to feed you when you come on a Sunday, to love you, to put our arms around you and help you in your marriage and family, and to equip you to *be* the church so that you can continue to be a minister in the marketplace. Together this is how we can build the kingdom of God. God is sending ordinary people out into the community to do extraordinary things!

Hebrews chapter 11 lists seventeen heroes of the faith. If you look you will see that sixteen of the people listed were working men and women. Only one of them was remotely involved in the work of the priesthood. Read the book of Acts and you will see that to achieve His purposes for the growth and establishment of the Church, God used a retailer, a paid soldier, a fashion dealer, an international finance minister, a prison warden, and two people in manufacturing. Five of the original apostles in the book of Acts were men who worked part time in other jobs!

The Bible itself was not written to theologians, nor is it written exclusively to church leaders. It is inspired and written for working men and women in everyday life. The New Testament was not written in high, academic Greek, but in "common" Greek, the language of the man in the street, so that ordinary people could understand and grasp its message.

> "...the purpose of the Church is realized in its fullness through ordinary people like us. God desires to work with everyone who is willing, with people who will wake up each morning excited about the possibilities of what He can and will do through them to build His kingdom."

I'm not sure where we got this weird idea that you are not a "real" minister unless you are employed and paid by the Church, but we need to redefine our perception of what it is to be a minister. This view of church hierarchy and structure has permeated the Church for far too long. We need to recapture the understanding that all of us are the Church and are equal partners in this thing we call ministry. Every one of us is a minister of the Gospel with no exceptions. We are all called and equipped by the Holy Spirit to transform the world in which we live daily.

The answer to the question, "Who is God sending?" is simply "us"! You and me. God is not just into using "superstars", although He can and will, but the purpose of the Church is realized in its fullness through ordinary people like us. God desires to work with everyone who is willing, with people who will wake up each morning excited about the possibilities of what He can and will do through them to build His kingdom.

What Will Be the Result?

If we cooperate with God's purposes the result will be that the salt will be poured out of the shaker and will begin to season our communities with the love and light of Christ.

Some time ago God took me to a passage of Scripture in Zechariah chapter 8. He showed me a prophetic picture of what a community looks like when the people of God begin to exert their influence on it.

> *"Then another message came to me from the* LORD *of Heaven's Armies: 'This is what the* LORD *of Heaven's Armies says: My love for Mount Zion is passionate and strong; I am consumed with passion for Jerusalem! And now the* LORD *says: I am returning to Mount Zion, and I will live in Jerusalem. Then Jerusalem will be called the Faithful City; the mountain of the* LORD *of Heaven's Armies will be called the Holy Mountain. This is what the* LORD *of Heaven's Armies says: Once again old men and women will walk Jerusalem's streets with their canes and will sit together in the city squares. And the streets of the city will be filled with boys and girls at play.'"*
>
> (ZECHARIAH 8:1–5)

God really impressed the principles in this verse on my heart and helped me to see what can happen when His people invite His presence into the midst of their city. My vision is that our kids will sit with the older generations; that older people with their walking canes will sit safely in our parks; our children will play safely in the streets; where there once was fear and desperation there will be a sense of hope and destiny.

In the verses above it is promised that Jerusalem's streets will once again be peaceful. I want to be bold enough to believe that for my city and yours too. It can happen if we, the Church, begin to be the salt seasoning our world. We can see a godly peace for our city brought about by a return to biblical truth that transforms communities. Can you see it? God says in Zechariah 8:6,

> *"All this may seem impossible to you now, a small remnant of God's people. But is it impossible for me? says the LORD of Heaven's Armies."*

Then God promises,

> *"You can be sure that I will rescue my people from the east and from the west. I will bring them home again to live safely in Jerusalem. They will be my people, and I will be faithful and just toward them as their God ... For I am planting seeds of peace and prosperity among you. The grapevines will be heavy with fruit. The earth will produce its crops, and the heavens will release the dew. Once more I will cause the remnant in Judah and Israel to inherit these blessings ... In those days ten men from different nations and languages of the world will clutch at the sleeve of one Jew. And they will say, 'Please let us walk with you, for we have heard that God is with you.'"*
>
> (ZECHARIAH 8:7–8, 12, 23)

What an incredible scripture! I long to see the same blessing of God in our own community. Remember the story of the crippled man who was healed when his friends lowered him down through the roof in front of Jesus (see Luke 5:18–20)? The Bible says that, *"When Jesus saw their faith, he said, 'Friend, your sins are forgiven'"* (v. 20) and the man was healed instantly. Notice that Jesus referred to "their faith" not the crippled man's faith. God wants us to believe for those who cannot believe for themselves, to have the kind of faith that will carry broken people the extra mile to the feet of Jesus, to climb on the roof and make a mess just so that one life can be changed. Our mission is to carry a crippled generation to Jesus Christ. We need to develop a culture in our churches that will flow out to our communities and reach the hurting and broken: those who are single and lonely, those who have been devastated by divorce, those who have been sexually abused.

> "God has a unique purpose and mission specifically for us. It would be a tragedy for us to head off to Africa to provide relief and somehow miss the mission field on our very doorstep."

The story is told of a wealthy Christian lady who had so much money that she didn't know what to do with it. She wondered, "What can I do with my money?" and she thought about going to Calcutta to help Mother Teresa's ministry. She wrote to Mother Teresa and waited to hear back. A short time later she received a letter which simply said: "Dear Mrs. A, please go and find your own Calcutta."

I believe the word of the Lord to His Church right now is that each and every church and Christian should "please go and find your own Calcutta." There is no point jumping on someone else's bandwagon, no matter how worthy the cause. We don't need to pursue someone else's mission, because God has a unique purpose and mission specifically for us. It would be a tragedy for us to head off to Africa to provide relief and somehow miss the mission field on our very doorstep. If we don't help the abused and rejected in our own community and instead fantasize about helping people in other nations, well, I can't help but feel that we missed the point. It's not an either/or situation. Let's build churches that seek to minister to the nations, absolutely, but let's also build churches that are aware of and willing to cross the street and meet the needs in front of us.

There are so many broken lives surrounding us every day and so many opportunities to be Jesus in even the most basic ways. We can be fathers to the fatherless, we can minister to broken children who need somebody to love them, to widows, orphans, prisoners, the elderly ... and we don't need unlimited funds or resources to do it. All we need is eyes that are open and a heart that understands what a wonderful place our world will be if the Church could look like that.

The heart of Sunday-Monday Church is a group of people who love God, worship Him together and are committed to growth, each one armed with the understanding that, "Come Monday, I am the church wherever I am. Whatever I'm doing I have the opportunity to touch and transform my surroundings." When we live like that the world around us will take notice. People want to know if we are for real and if this stuff can really work.

GROWING IN INFLUENCE

As we continue to reach out and love our community in practical, tangible ways, we will grow in influence as the people of God. And as we are faithful in serving others in small ways God will give us greater opportunities to speak into the lives of those in positions of power and influence within society.

Some time ago, unexpectedly, I received a call from a politician who had won a seat in the south east of our city. I had never met him before. My mind immediately went back to a prophecy I had received years before. A great friend of mine, an Assemblies of God leader from the UK, had prophesied over me that God would bring about a day when I would have the opportunity to influence the leaders of our community and that they would come looking for me. Not long after this first "surprise" phone call, another of our city's influential politicians called me, having heard some of the Monday church things we were doing in our community. "I'm hearing so much about your church and the many ways it's reaching the community," he said. "I'm about to go to Canberra to be with the Prime Minister. I'd like you to give me a list of any needs you have because I'll be talking with the PM about community services." It is an incredibly humbling experience to begin to see the favour of God as you step out in obedience. It wasn't my great leadership or charisma that brought about favour with government, it was simply allowing my Sunday world to begin affecting my Monday world.

God is doing a unique thing through His Church to touch those in authority in our communities. Recently, while ministering in Brisbane, I had a similar prophetic word for a young pastor. This pastor had expressed a fervent desire to build a church that has the Sunday-Monday balance God is speaking about. During my visit God really impressed on my heart a specific and unusual word which wouldn't leave me: "The community is going to come to you and ask you, 'Why is your church so successful?' and 'Can you help us with families in our community?'" Already having such a burden in his heart to see his community transformed, tears streamed down this young man's face as I prayed over him.

Shortly afterwards I received an excited phone call from him. A few days after I had prayed for him a reporter from the main Brisbane newspaper had come to the church asking to see him. The reporter had told him, "We want to do a story on 'family' in the paper, but we are struggling to find a good family that is still together! Then we heard about you. Can we do a story on you? And could you tell us all about your church too?" The story made the front page of the Brisbane newspaper. God is alive and moving in His Church!

PART TWO

SUNDAY MONDAY
CHURCH

CHAPTER 3

SUNDAY AND MONDAY CHURCH WORKING TOGETHER

I believe the thing that we, the Church, really need to grasp at this time is the need for *balance*. Without powerful Sunday church our Monday church expressions will likely lack the purpose and effectiveness we so desire to see. But if the expression of Monday church is absent, then our Sunday church will become an unhealthy place to be because we will be isolated and irrelevant. God's ideal is that we have *both* elements working in harmony, it should never be an either/or thing. So many Christian organisations have pursued a social transformation ministry that is detached from the power of effective Sunday Church and the result has almost always been the same: they become disconnected from the rest of the Body of Christ. While many of the things they achieve are great, it leaves me wondering what might have been had they attached it to the person and power of Jesus and linked that to who we, the Church, are called to be.

Without the Sunday-Monday Church connection our Monday church activities will only ever minister to the practical issues in people's lives, ignoring the spiritual. Yet God has given us the potential to do so much more. If our "ministry" lacks any spiritual content then it might as well be coming from any humanitarian organisation looking to do good in the world. Monday church minus Sunday church does not have the ability to attract people into the kingdom of God. Neither does it address the most fundamental of all human needs: the need for a relationship with God. Sunday church and Monday church have to work together in partnership, otherwise people will lose out.

> **"Sunday church worship is about
> lifting our hands up.
> Monday church worship is about
> reaching our hands out."**

Here is a quick comparison of the Sunday church/Monday church paradigms that illustrates that, whilst they are distinctly different, they bring balance to each other:

- Sunday church is about believers. Monday church is about not-yet-believers.

- Sunday church is about discipling people. Monday church is about demonstrating the Gospel in the community.
- Sunday church is about revelation. Monday church is about activation.
- Sunday church is predominantly built by Ephesians 4:11 giftings. Monday church is built by the whole congregation with everyone doing their part.
- Sunday church worship is about lifting our hands up. Monday church worship is about reaching our hands out.
- Sunday church is about teaching and equipping. Monday church is about doing.
- Sunday church is about listening to God. Monday church is about listening to others.
- Sunday church is about coming. Monday church is about going.
- Sunday church feeds us so we can grow. Monday church feeds others so they can live.
- Sunday church is about growing in our faith. Monday church is about going to the faithless.
- Sunday church is about coming to family. Monday church is about going to the fatherless.

We have discussed the fact that Sunday church is primarily built through the effective operation of the Ephesians 4:11 ministry gifts of apostles, prophets, evangelists, pastors and teachers, and that its primary purpose is to encourage, equip and build up the lives of our people. This needs to happen in order to keep the people of God fuelled for purpose and moving in the right direction (though we do need to be careful that this does not become an excuse for people to sit back and be inactive in the life of the church). Monday church, however, is not primarily built by the Ephesians 4 giftings, but more often than not by the giftings listed in Romans 12 that each of us possesses in different degrees:

"In his grace, God has given us different gifts for doing certain things well. So if God has given you the ability to prophesy, speak out with as much faith as God has given you. If your gift is serving others, serve them well. If you are a teacher, teach well. If your gift is to encourage others, be encouraging. If it is giving, give generously. If God has given you leadership ability, take the responsibility seriously. And if you have a gift for showing kindness to others, do it gladly."

(ROMANS 12:6–8)

As well as prophecy and teaching (which also appear in the Ephesians 4:11 list, but with a different emphasis) Paul identifies the gifts of serving, encouraging, giving financially, leading and showing kindness – gifts that are vital for resourcing and building Monday church.

Sunday church is about worship, about lifting our hands up to God to praise and honour Him. Monday church is about worship too, but about making our *work* an act of worship and reaching out to others. We must aspire to be Christians who not only love to raise our hands in worship to God, but who also have a deep desire to stretch out our hands to others. We must have both aspects otherwise our spiritual life is out of balance.

It's great to have Sunday church that teaches and equips believers, but without a deliberate plan of attack it is human nature for us to look for a place of comfort. So many of our congregations get stuck in a cozy comfort zone and never move out of it. If our focus is only on teaching instead of sending people out to be salt and light in their workplaces, well we are equipped ... but equipped for what?

The Christian walk can be broken down into seven distinct stages that should chart our journey towards spiritual maturity. These are probably best left as the subject of a different book, but in summary they look like this:

- We begin with *comfort* as we come to Christ.
- From comfort we move to *connection* as we begin to embrace the people and values of the kingdom.
- Through our connection we become aware of the *cause* as we begin to see our Christian life in the greater context of the mission of the Church.
- The cause brings us to a place of *commitment* as we decide to play our part in the greater context.
- Once we begin to get committed it's generally only a short time before life will send *crisis* our way as our faith is tested.
- Through crisis we move to a place of *conviction* as our core values are firmly established.
- Finally, through a life driven by our convictions, we reap a lifestyle of *consistency*.

> **"If we can help people to transition through these stages to reach a place of maturity in their Christian life we will see less people living on the fringe of the church and more people gripped by the cause of Christ..."**

The challenge we have as the Church is that most of us really enjoy stages one and two. We like comfort and connection! Some of us even enjoy the cause, but very few of us feel the same way about commitment. Commitment is never really tested until you don't feel like doing something. Up until then it's just agreement. The real test is whether we will live our life to fulfil the cause that God has given us.

If we can help people to transition through these stages to reach a place of maturity in their Christian life we will see less people living on the fringe of the church and more people gripped by the cause of Christ, willing to take hold of all they were designed to be. This is the task of Sunday church. Not only that, but as we give people a cause to motivate them, we will see fewer people leaving our churches to go and look for other churches when the sense of comfort and connection no longer seems quite so compelling as it once was. In Western Church culture this habit of migrating to another church when things don't suit us any more has reached almost epidemic proportions and it causes me in many ways to feel the regret of "what if?" What if we had been able to teach our people how to successfully negotiate these seasons of maturity? How different would things look then? But despite that I know that we are faced with the opportunity to change *now*, to help people navigate their journey successfully and to transition from being people who attend church services to becoming powerful people living lives driven by conviction.

SEEING THE BIGGER PICTURE

Most of us live busy lives and your church life is probably just as hectic as the other areas of your life. For that reason it's good to step back and take stock of what our church activities are really producing or accomplishing. We especially need to see the bigger picture in terms of what God is doing and see how we fit into His plans.

A few years ago God spoke a particular word into my heart. It got my attention because it seemed a strange thing for God to say. "I'm stuck!", He said. Can you ever imagine God being stuck? "How does God get stuck?" I thought. I sought further clarification and I felt God say quite clearly, "I can't build My Church with angels, I can only build it with broken humanity. I'm stuck with what you give Me."

It's true. God can only build with the raw materials we give Him. He won't supernaturally bypass us and suddenly bring revival to the Church. He is committed to using you and me in all our brokenness. That's why it is so important that we listen to His voice and cooperate when He tells us to do something.

Before our own church could embark upon a program of radical change that would see us move towards a healthier balance between Sunday and Monday church, I needed to see the bigger picture myself. As is usually the case when God is moving you to something new, it often begins with Him leading you to do something you wouldn't ordinarily do! He challenged me to go to a particular conference run by a church in our area. I immediately said to the Lord, "This is so far outside my comfort zone, God. I don't need to be in another meeting." But I felt the Spirit of God challenge me saying, "You need to go to something that is totally different to you, because I want you to find Me there." So my wife, Sharonne, and I found ourselves driving to this conference.

We pulled up at the venue and all I can say is that I have never met such grumpy car park assistants in my life! We eventually made our way into the auditorium and looked for a seat. Nobody spoke to us at all and I felt God say to me, "Now you know how other people feel sometimes when they come to your church." That was good for my pride, I can tell you! The only available seats were right at the back and God said to me, "Now you know how other people feel when they come late to your church and can't get a seat." I began to realize at this point, through these simple things, that as great as our church is, this must be what it feels like for a new person. It was a really intimidating and daunting experience. I knew we needed to change.

At the conference that day I learned a valuable lesson: that every expression of the Body of Christ is valid and that we all need to work together and not allow our different expressions to keep us from seeing the bigger picture. God helped me to see that, unwittingly, I had been almost oblivious to what other parts of His Church were doing, simply because they did it differently from us. God said to me, "Danny, we can no longer afford to draw lines in the sand based on music or style. Every time you do it's like you are cutting your own finger off." There are so many different expressions of the Body of Christ, many different, diverse parts to it, but it is still His Body.

This experience so opened my eyes that as I was reading the New Testament, it suddenly struck me how God never speaks to a single church or local body, He always addresses the *collective* Church in a city. All throughout the New Testament God spoke to geographic locations where all the believers were together. The churches in that region may have been quite different from one another in character, all with different emphases, different styles of worship etc., but God seemed to be able to see past all that – it was just His Church, a part of His Body gathered together in a certain location. That is how we should view the Body of Christ too.

Not "Either/Or" but "Both"

The next step, once I realized this, and as God began to speak to me about the direction our church would take, was to find a way to get these two expressions to operate in harmony with each other – Sunday and Monday church, working together. It could not be an "either/or" thing, we had to have both elements functioning in partnership with one another. Yes, we needed to get the "salt out of the shaker" to do its work in the community, but we still needed a shaker!

The trap many churches fall into is that of becoming so engrossed in looking after and enhancing what they've got that they fail to truly listen to what God is saying or to look outwards. We're get so concerned with our "salt shaker" – how great it is and how we can enhance it – that we forget to shake the salt out of it to do its work. How crazy is that?

"Look at our shaker," we say. "We've got giant plasma screens and a fountain outside!" I so believe in doing church with a spirit of excellence, but if it comes down to a choice between that and feeding hungry people, does God really care about our plasma screens? We have to break our preoccupation with what goes on just within our own walls.

We have also been sold the lie that we have to get Sunday church "right" before we can attempt Monday church. Once, after I had preached on this subject at a meeting on the Gold Coast, a pastor came up to me and said, "Danny, it's great what your church is doing and I appreciate your message, but most of our churches are still struggling. I don't know how we can focus more on Monday church until we get that right. I don't know if we're ready for this message."

> **"I so believe in doing church with a spirit of excellence, but if it comes down to a choice between that and feeding hungry people, does God really care about our plasma screens? We have to break our preoccupation with what goes on just within our own walls."**

Straightaway I knew the answer: "God doesn't want you to and He shouldn't have to choose. He wants both expressions of church. But I think if He had to choose, He would rather have a church of 40 people who are in their local community feeding the poor, being a light in the darkness, than a megachurch with great teaching and endless resources for its members."

The Bible says in John 3:16, *"For God so loved the world..."*. It doesn't say, "For God so loved the Church...". Although we know God does indeed love the Church, as Christians we are called to be lights in a dark world. Lights are relatively ineffective in well lit places. So where would the light of your and my life be better utilized, in a dark world or a well lit church? I believe God would rather have out-of-tune worship on a Sunday that comes from hearts fully committed to seeking the lost than an unbelievable choir and an awesome worship band who produce great sounding worship but are indifferent to the needs of broken humanity.

I strongly believe in excellence in the Church and I hold the conviction that it's part of what the Church is designed to be. But we cannot allow ourselves to become the victims of our own success. The worship in our churches can be fantastic, but it is missing the mark if it mostly succeeds in attracting bored Christians from other churches who are looking for something fresh.

But equally, we cannot build Monday church to the exclusion of Sunday church. If we do that we will become separated from our source and our saltiness will quickly disappear. We will become *social* but not *spiritual*. Our aim in building Monday church in our community has to be a desire to demonstrate the conviction we hold that Jesus is the truth *by our actions*.

Sure there are heaps of arguments for and against the emphasis on either Sunday or Monday church, but what really counts is what God wants and what really works in reaching people. If you were to stop a completely un-churched person in the street and ask them what they thought about the Salvation Army, for instance, the overwhelming response would be a positive one. For the majority of people they are most visible representation of Christ they can think of. People recognise the fact that they are out there actually doing good for other people! Plus they can see that their faith is closely linked to their actions.

Of course, the criticism most often levelled at those churches who are passionate about Monday church is that they are taking away the emphasis from Sunday church and actually weakening the Body. My experience has been that the reverse is true. I am not campaigning for Monday church in and of itself, I just want to see what will happen if we can get the Sunday-Monday church balance I believe God is calling for.

As is often the case wherever people are involved, when we get excited about something we are often guilty of throwing out the old in favour of the new, jumping on the bandwagon of the latest, greatest fad. Herein lies the danger as we come to a fresh understanding about Monday church. We must never use it as an excuse to abandon Sunday church. I have heard people say things like, "My ministry is out there in the community." That may well be true, but it does not mean that Sunday church is no longer relevant.

All of us who are enjoying the benefits of a real and vibrant relationship with God hunger to be in His house anyway. But as Christians it is so important that we are part of, and regularly attending, a local church, because this is the place where we can be refuelled, energised, challenged and receive the tools that will equip us for the ministry we engage in Monday to Friday.

I remember attending a meeting at a friend's church in Sydney and chatting to a very successful Christian businessman and friend. I commented to him, "You're a really busy guy, but you always seem to be in church. When do you find the time to run your business?" He said to me, "I can't afford *not* to be in the house of God. Sunday fuels me for what God has called me to do!" Perhaps there is a principle to be learned here.

Who Builds Monday Church?

In the light of this new way of doing things and all the repercussions of it God began challenging me to work systematically through the book of Matthew. Looking at the text

> "Jesus was committed to a model of Church
> that combined both practical action
> and spiritual power."

in the context of Sunday-Monday church it is immediately obvious that Jesus was firmly focused on impacting His community. He was much more concerned with the impact God's kingdom could make on society than He was with the established Church, a fact illustrated quite clearly as we look at this brief summary of the book:

- *Chapter 1*: Jesus was born in the community – literally. He wasn't born in a church or a hospital, but in the community, in fact on the premises of a business – an inn owned by a local inn keeper!
- *Chapter 2*: Jesus lived in the community in a town called Nazareth.
- *Chapter 3*: Jesus was confirmed to be the Christ, not in church at an ordination service, but in the Judean wilderness by John the Baptist.
- *Chapter 4*: Jesus was tested in the wilderness, not in a worship centre.

  Many of the tests that come our way in life won't happen in church. For many years now I have taught the following with regard to people's calling: Jesus **reveals**, **reverses** and **restores**. Jesus will reveal a calling on your life and then, in your Monday to Friday world, you will be tested to see if you can fulfil that calling. You will also go through "reversals"; i.e. if you promise God you are going to serve Him, invariably your resolve will be tested. Things like this always happen because when God calls you to higher ground He is also committed to sifting out of you all that would hinder your progress. You have to shed the dead weight in your life that could hold you back and this process includes refining your character. If you don't pass the tests in the wilderness of everyday life then God won't release you into your full potential, simply because it's a place that you don't yet have the capacity to deal with effectively.

- *Chapter 5*: Jesus preached the greatest sermon He ever preached, not in a church, but on a mountain top.
- *Chapters 6 & 7*: Jesus taught about various topics, all of which were to do with everyday life in the community: law, sexuality, marriage, making and breaking oaths, revenge, loving your enemies, money and possessions. He was teaching about life. It's so important that we follow Jesus' example in this and teach our people things that are going to help them live their lives, that will help them in their marriages and homes. We need to preach the stuff that the Bible *is* clear on and we need to teach people how to do life.
- *Chapter 8*: Jesus begins healing people in their homes or out in the streets; e.g. a Roman Centurion at his house and Peter's mother-in-law at his home.
- *Chapter 9*: Jesus calls Matthew into ministry when He is just walking down the road. There is no special ordination service, it all happens on the road.
- *Chapter 10*: Jesus' disciples are sent into the community.
- *Chapter 11*: Jesus goes Himself into towns and cities.
- *Chapter 12*: In this chapter the religious people start arguing about how to do church!
- *Chapter 13*: Jesus begins telling stories about farming and agriculture that are relevant to the life and work of those listening to Him.
- *Chapter 14*: Jesus feeds 5,000 people in a desolate place.
- *Chapter 15*: He feeds another 4,000 people.

- *Chapter 16*: Jesus says, "I will build my Church" and He wasn't in church when He said it, He was out in a field. We've got to get the message of what Church is. The Church is not bricks – it's us – you and me.
- *Chapter 17*: Jesus experiences transfiguration on a mountain, out in the open air.

    What better place could there be for the anointing to fall than whilst you are going about your work in the everyday world, working at the car manufacturing plant or talking to someone on your lunch break? Something happens to you and as a result your work colleagues want to know what's different about you. Right there you can have an encounter and "be" church.
- *Chapters 18 & 19*: Here Jesus teaches by calling children to Himself. What a wonderful picture. When everybody is busy wanting to do church, Jesus stops for the little children.
- *Chapter 20*: Jesus heals two blind men as He leaves Jericho.
- *Chapter 21*: Jesus clears the temple. He seeks to drive out of the Church everything that is false and corrupt.
- *Chapter 22*: Jesus talks about parties and refers to the Great Feast.
- *Chapter 23*: Jesus cries over the city of Jerusalem because He sees how lost it is.
- *Chapter 24*: Jesus does a great deal of His teaching after leaving the temple grounds. How much teaching do we do after we leave the temple grounds, after we're outside church? We often come to church and are impacted by the teaching, but great teaching is only evidenced by what it activates in us. When we leave the church carrying what we have heard in the "temple" to the mission fields of our daily lives – that's when we'll see miraculous things begin to happen in our community.
- *Chapter 25*: Jesus talks about investment and the kingdom.

- *Chapter 26*: Jesus conducts the last supper with His disciples. It's not a church service, it happens at someone's house.
- *Chapter 27*: Jesus is crucified before a crowd out in the open.
- *Chapter 28*: Jesus tells us to, *"Go and make disciples of all nations."*

What seems so clear as we look at the themes highlighted is that Jesus was committed to a model of Church that combined both practical action and spiritual power. He would build His Church and it would be founded upon the power of the kingdom of God and the miraculous. Needy and desperate people would be touched as Jesus met them where they were. That is Monday church and Sunday church working together in harmony. When our churches look like that then we will see the Church have the kind of impact that we all long for.

CHAPTER 4

HOW WE BEGAN TO BUILD MONDAY CHURCH

As God spoke to me more and more about building Monday church, I began to think about what that would look like. What could we do that would make a significant impact on our community? It had to be something that would be of great benefit and a blessing to the community and at the same time communicate the message that the Christians in our region care about their community.

One of the first things on my heart was to do something for the Adelaide Children's Hospital. I thought, "What an impact it could have on the lives of so many families struggling through the worst time of their lives." I began to wonder, what if the Christians of South Australia pooled their resources and worked together to set about renovating the hospital – what kind of message would that send to the community? The vision that began to burn in my heart was one of seeing a group of churches, all partnering together to tackle the project. That way, the initiative could not be attributed to any one particular church, group or denomination. It would have to be about more than that and as a result Jesus would be glorified. If the media wanted to talk about the event they would have to say something like, "The churches of Adelaide..." or "The Christians of Adelaide have come together to do this..."

I felt that it was a "God project", but as with most things, timing is everything and the timing wasn't initially right for something of that magnitude. I knew that it was something He had put in *my* heart, but wanting further confirmation from God that this was the type of thing we were supposed to be doing I prayed, "Speak this into somebody else's heart too, Lord."

Soon after I prayed the prayer, I arrived home to find that someone had anonymously deposited an article in my post box. I never found out who sent it to me. The article was written by an American pastor, Eric Swanson, who I'd not heard of before, and was entitled, "Ten paradigm shifts towards community transformation". The title alone was almost enough for me, but as I sat down and began reading the article, everything that God had put on my heart, that I had been speaking about to our church for the last two years, was summed up in black and white. In fact, though I'd never read the article before or heard of the pastor, anyone who read it might well have said, "Aha, so this is where he got it all from!"

The ten paradigm shifts outlined in the article are listed below. They outline some of the necessary steps we need to take for our churches to see Monday church functioning well. The Church must move from...

1. ... building walls to building bridges
2. ... measuring attendance to measuring impact
3. ... encouraging the saints to attend the service to equipping the saints for working service
4. ... "serve us" to "service" – from inward to outward focus
5. ... duplication of human services and ministries to partnering with existing services and ministries
6. ... fellowship to functional unity
7. ... condemning the city to blessing the city and praying for it
8. ... being a minister in a congregation to being a minister in a parish
9. ... anecdote and speculation to valid information
10. ... teacher to learner

In his article, Swanson writes about the following case study:

"Erwin McManus of Mosaic Church in East Los Angeles says that the single biggest factor in his church retaining people is not personal follow-up or joining a small group; it is being involved from the very beginning in service to others in the community. When members have told him that they want the church to meet their needs his reply is, 'You ARE the church and together we are called to meet the needs of the world.' Over 1,800 members agree: we grow and are healed as we serve others. Maybe this is what Isaiah (58:6–8) had in mind when he penned God's words to his people: *'Is this not the kind of fasting I have chosen: To loose the chains of injustice and untie the cords of the yoke, to set the oppressed free and break every yoke? Is it not to share your food with the hungry and to provide the poor wanderer with shelter...? Then your light will break forth like the dawn and **your healing will quickly appear**.'* What if we settled for nothing less than 100% of our church members engaged at some level in meaningful ministry to the community? People (or small groups) could choose their field and level of engagement (from once a week to once a year), but non-involvement would not be an option."

Swanson's article was exactly what I needed to confirm the things God had put on my heart, and I knew it was time to make a start. The Children's Hospital was a project I knew would happen in time, but I felt it right that we make a start in our own local community by contacting one of our local High Schools with an offer to renovate it. I felt God say to me, "This is just the beginning." Over the course of two weekends somewhere in the region of 700 volunteers partnered with local businesses in a complete makeover worth hundreds of thousands of dollars. The impact it had on the school was great, but it also had a profound impact on our church! All of a sudden we were reinvigorated by the joy we felt at not just attending church, but being the Church. However, the impact was to be wider still. As I write, I know of hundreds of schools around the world that have been renovated by Christians in their local communities as a result of hearing about what we did. What a great example of how God can take one act of obedience and use it to transform thousands of lives!

> "...this was about *the* Church not *our* church. I knew that God wanted to bring about a faceless revival."

After we completed the school project we really felt it was just the beginning and it wasn't long before we felt the Lord saying, "Now it's time to tackle the Women's and Children's Hospital." Despite some initial opposition, we spoke to the people who ran the hospital and they were delighted, even amazed and a little sceptical, that we were interested in helping them renovate their building. In the past they had received some help from celebrities who had made one-off donations or fronted fundraising events, but that was all, and most of those people wanted to buy equipment for the hospital. What we wanted to do was to renovate large sections of it where the state of the rooms was little better than a run-down prison.

In our discussions with the hospital it was decided that we should work on some rooms which were set apart for parents who had kids in long-term care. These rooms were primarily for use by families with kids battling cancer so that they could constantly be near to them. The hospital board also asked if we would consider planting some gardens where people could go and pray. Of course, we said yes and already our Monday church was making way for our Sunday church. Some time later the director of the hospital came to a church service on Sunday morning and told everyone how excited he was to be partnering with us.

We probably could have easily managed a project like this on our own. After undertaking a project like the High School this was actually quite a bit smaller, but that wasn't the vision. If we had gone down that road, then it would have been conflicting with the very principles I believed God was working to establish. We would have received all the recognition and could have very much enhanced our own image, but this was about *the* Church not *our* church. I knew that God wanted to bring about a faceless revival. He wanted the Christians of Adelaide to rise up and work together as one, activated to be the Church.

Even the school and hospital were just the beginning. We moved on to work in the women's prison in Adelaide where we carried out major renovations throughout the prison. Some people could take the view, "But, they're prisoners! They're in prison because they've done something wrong. Why make it comfortable for them?" All I know is, numbers of prisoners came to Christ whilst inside as a result of the initiative. We see them as the Church outside of our walls. If it was good enough for Jesus to say, "I was in prison and you visited me" then I guess it is something He feels is important and we need to look after those people and give them fresh hope.

> "It benefits us very little claiming to be a follower of Christ and saying all the right things if we fail to bear it out in our actions. These actions – caring for the marginalised and disenfranchised in society – are the actions that are really important to God."

Churches putting aside their differences, working together in a city to accomplish things for God, is such a simple yet powerful equation. Imagine if fifty churches gave just $1,000 each towards a joint-church project – that's $50,000 easily raised to kick-start the budget. Having demonstrated their resolve it would then be much easier for churches to persuade local or even national companies to come on board and donate services or materials such as carpeting, paint, furniture etc. Each "partner" in the venture would be contributing something fairly modest, but the impact of the whole working together would be very significant.

I would find it sad if all the Church ever did was spend our resources on staging conferences with big name speakers to attract the crowds, rather than engaging in endeavours that would directly touch the lives of unbelievers. I'm not against people coming together to hear great preaching, because we need to have our Sunday church focus. The problem I have is when I see Sunday church being built to the exclusion of Monday church. Our Christianity has to be real if it means anything at all. Remember these well known verses from James chapter 1:

> *"If you claim to be religious but don't control your tongue, you are fooling yourself, and your religion is worthless. Pure and genuine religion in the sight of God the Father means caring for orphans and widows in their distress and refusing to let the world corrupt you."*

(JAMES 1:26–27)

Notice how the apostle James links together the use of our tongues with the act of reaching out to the poor. It benefits us very little claiming to be a follower of Christ and saying all the right things if we fail to bear it out in our actions. These actions – caring for the marginalised and disenfranchised in society – are the actions that are really important to God. James teaches that our mouths determine our manner. The things that we talk about and the beliefs we continually express determine what we do with our lives. Selfish Christianity flows from the selfish speech of a selfish heart. Our tongues have the power to change the world, but it's so much easier to get busy complaining and backbiting instead of speaking about kingdom matters. We need to practise speaking out kingdom values.

When I first started our church some years ago, someone came to me and said, "You need to change your motto because you're not doing anything that your motto says you are doing." My response was, "You know what, you're right, but I refuse to camp there. We need to *speak into* what we are becoming!" Unless we first declare our intentions before God, our actions will never catch up.

James goes on to say,

"What good is it, dear brothers and sisters, if you say you have faith but don't show it by your actions? Can that kind of faith save anyone?"

(JAMES 2:14)

What's the use of having faith (an expression of Sunday church), James says, if you don't prove it by your actions (an expression of Monday church)? That kind of faith can't save anyone. Jesus warned against being the type of Christian who sees a brother or sister in need of food or clothing and does nothing for them except to say, "God bless you, stay warm and eat well." What good does that do? Faith that doesn't show itself through good deeds is dead and useless. Incidentally, we tend to apply those words of Jesus – "brother or sister" – to our fellow Christians, but I am convinced Jesus meant it to be applied much more widely than that, so that it includes our fellow human beings regardless of their beliefs, wherever we might find them in need.

The classic argument, which I have heard countless times and that seems to stop many people from engaging in Monday church is, "Some people's ministry is meant to be in the Church, and some people's ministry is meant to be outside." They are taking a fragment of what James said out of context: "Some have faith [Sunday church] and others have good deeds [Monday church]" because he goes on to say that our faith is actually demonstrated by our good works. But there is a seed of truth in this argument which is why it sounds convincing. Some people's gifts may well be better put to use inside rather than outside of the Church. But that does not mean that we are absolved of any responsibility to reach out to those in our community. James' teaching clearly counters such a view saying, in effect, "I can't see your faith *at all* unless you have good deeds

70

being worked out as a result of it." There is much talk today about impacting our cities for Christ and changing history. I believe the church that will impact its city the most, and therefore change history, will be the one that fully embraces both Sunday and Monday church and sees both paradigms working together in harmony to fulfil God's kingdom purposes in their location.

PAYING THE PRICE OF CHANGE

I believe anything that's valuable costs something and anyone who wants to see God move in power and impact their city has to be willing to pay the price to see that happen. Prayer is a big part of that price, but action is part of it too. I have often been asked, "Why don't we see many miracles in the Western Church?" I believe it is largely due to the fact that, in many cases, we are unwilling to pay the high price required to see them. We live a life of divided loyalty, torn by the comforts of our Western lifestyle. What if we were to get desperate? What if we began to petition God day and night for a breakthrough until we got it? Think about the possibilities of that kind of desperation.

The instructions of the Bible are simple: *"Seek first the kingdom of God..."* We could learn a lesson from the Muslim faith in this regard: we have prayer "meetings" while they have a prayer "culture". In the same way we need to create a Monday church *culture* in our congregations as opposed to running "programs" or "initiatives". At our own church we have endeavoured to cut back the number of meetings that take place during the week so that our people are able to "do life" in their community. In other words, we are doing all we can to get the salt out of the shaker so it can do its job, seasoning and preserving wherever it is placed.

From experience I can say that the effect of this has been to place a greater importance and emphasis on our Sunday meetings than ever before. It has not weakened the church in any way. Rather than diverting attention away from the Sunday church paradigm, as some might expect, it has become more focused – a time to resource, refresh and reinvigorate people with the best teaching available. It is also a time where we can give and draw encouragement from one another as Hebrews 10:24 instructs,

> *"Let us think of ways to motivate one another to acts of love and good works."*

The NKJV translates this verse: *"Let us consider one another in order to stir up love and good works."* The original Greek phrase that is translated "stir up" means "to motivate" and actually carries the sense of putting your foot on someone's backside and giving them a good shove! Our English translations have sanitised the impact of the original words, but the intention is that we strongly exhort one another saying, "Come on! Let's do this thing!" This is a key function of Sunday church – to exhort one another to get back out there on Monday and do the business of the kingdom.

EXPRESSIONS OF MONDAY CHURCH

Sunday church is built by individual groups of believers with different styles and different emphases. We are all allowed to do church in accordance with our personal convictions as to what is pleasing to God and relevant to those we are called to reach. Some people will have a more reflective style while others will have an upfront, in-your-face style. God is a God of variety! He accepts and encourages diversity in our worship of Him. God encourages us to build our local gatherings according to our convictions, so each one will be quite different, but each one is a valid expression of God's collective Body. Churches may be part of a denominational structure or an informal, relational network. It doesn't really matter as long as the life of God is in them.

> "The bottom line is: if we are going to see revival in our cities, it will be when we put aside our differences and mistrust and work together as the Body of Christ for a common cause."

Monday church, however, is not concerned with denominations or other formal/informal structures. It is concerned only with a demonstration of the Gospel in the community. Monday church is built by individuals who belong to the whole Body of Christ – from individual churches, streams or denominations – who will work together in their city to bring about a faceless revival. As I mentioned earlier, God's ultimate for Monday church is that when the newspapers report on what the people of God are doing in their city, they can't say that it's down to your church or my church, they have to say it's just "Christians" working together. The bottom line is: if we are going to see revival in our cities, it will be when we put aside our differences and mistrust and work together as the Body of Christ for a common cause.

Monday church is built by people who have seen beyond the boundaries of their church walls and have caught something of God's heart for the lost and hurting. I can think of no better example of Monday church people than a particular couple in our church who exemplify this mindset and attitude.

Struggling with their daughter's own very serious condition and spending a great deal time at the Adelaide Women's and Children's Hospital, this incredible couple managed to see past the desperation of their own circumstances. Although their daughter was very ill, they still noticed another couple who were visiting their children at the same time. This couple had twins who were both very sick.

Seeing what a tough time the family appeared to be having and after learning, through some enquiries, that the husband had been forced to quit his job so he could spend time looking after his wife and children, Monday church began to be stirred in the heart of this couple. They saw how run down the family car had become due to the financial hardship faced by this family and the husband mentioned this to one of the pastors on our church staff who had been visiting with them at the hospital.

He in turn mentioned it at a church pastoral care leaders' meeting that evening. To his great surprise, as he spoke about this family's plight to the leaders, the group murmured amongst themselves for a few moments and then one of them spoke up: "We need to do something for these people, something practical. Let's buy them a car." Without any prompting from "leadership" they began to pass around the offering container in the hope of doing something practical for this family in desperate need. Monday church!

The events that unfolded next were quite amazing. Some of the leaders approached a local car dealer and when the situation was explained to him he was only too happy to give a massive discount on a vehicle for this couple. Another businessman heard about what was going on and said, "I would love to supply $500 worth of petrol for these people." Then someone who worked for an insurance company got wind of what was going on and said, "We'll provide comprehensive insurance for the car for a year to help get this family back on their feet." Completely overwhelmed by the kindness of their encounter with the church, it wasn't too long before this couple visited our church where they could experience the love of the family of God and hear the Gospel. Because the people of God had reached out to them, because they didn't wait for an event to invite them to but just met a need, this young family was changed forever and they wanted to be in church, even though they didn't know Christ yet.

During their darkest hour this couple from our church never lost sight of the fact that they *were* the church, they didn't just *attend* church. As a result not only was another family changed forever, but a lasting impact was made on the medical staff at the hospital who were caring for their daughter. So profound was their influence that when the husband said to one of the doctors, "We're so grateful for all you're doing for our daughter, my wife and I would love to take you out for a meal" the surgeon immediately replied, "I'd rather you take me to your church!" What an incredible statement! What a powerful demonstration of Monday church!

Even before we renovated a High School or a hospital our church became involved in helping a café in our local area. Feeling the burden to pastor our community, be community-minded and concentrate less on ourselves we were looking for any opportunity to begin to activate our Monday church focus. We knew it had to be God when the owners of the café contacted the church and asked for some information. Strangely enough, it wasn't our preaching or our music they had noticed, it was our colour scheme! They wanted to know if we had used an interior designer to create the feeling of warmth in our décor. They were more than a little surprised when we informed them we had come up with the ideas ourselves. Then came the open door: "Would you be willing to help us with some ideas?"

God had been so good in providing us with this opportunity we were determined to make something of it. We decided we would not only help them with their colour scheme, but we would organise a group of volunteers from the church to go in on a Sunday evening and work all through the night, so as to cause as little disruption to the running of the café as possible. Not only would we save them money by volunteering our labour and expertise, but we would invest into them by underwriting the cost of all the materials needed. Our desire really was to be a blessing to our community and here we were with an incredible opportunity to give of our time and resources – and to see to it that they did not lose one day of business in the process.

The cost to us as a church was fairly minimal – the sacrifice of some time and a few thousand dollars worth of materials. But the impact we made on the owners of the café was enormous. At times they would burst into tears of gratitude, questioning how and why we would do this. All we could say was that we knew that we were put in this community by God to be a blessing and this was just one of the ways we could show it. It wasn't about getting a free meal, it wasn't really even about getting them to come to church, it was more about changing their perception of who God was.

Great things were even happening even in the midst of the project. When we went to visit one of the local shops to buy some tiles the owner of the shop asked me, "What are you doing?" so I told him: "We're from the church and we're renovating the café as a gift to the people who run it." "Why?" he asked, "Well, I guess we want to show them that the church is not here trying to get something for nothing, but that our heart is really to try and put something back into the community we believe we are called to serve so that we bless people." The gentleman behind the counter was a little lost for words. Finally he said, "Freak me out!" and called his wife over to explain to her what we were doing. Then he said to her, "We've got to get on board with this. How much cheaper can we do it?" In the end, tiles that should have cost us in excess of $700 cost us around $250, but more importantly, someone else's perception of what the Church is was changed forever through Monday church!

All the things we have been led to do have created a level of trust and respect within our community that is a platform from which we can speak words about Jesus that will be listened to. Our actions have opened people's hearts and minds to the Gospel. We have reached out practically with the love of Christ and shown that our faith means something; that it can be outworked in real and tangible ways; it's not just a theory.

My connection with the owner of the café actually positioned me to speak into the life of someone else I wouldn't otherwise have met. On one occasion when I visited there I was introduced to the owner's sister. In the course of conversation I discovered that she had lost her husband and her son, both on the same day, in a tragic helicopter crash. I'm not sure what she really thought about God or Christianity, but nevertheless she told me that she felt that the people from our church would probably be the first ones to get into Heaven. I was then presented with the great privilege of being able to sit with her and share something of the love of God with her. All this because we were willing to paint some walls, do the unexpected and engage the people we are called to reach with unmerited, even "unnecessary" generosity. The Gospel is, after all, about reaching the lost, lonely and hurting, even through practical service.

In 1994 I wrote on a piece of paper, "The church I want to build will restore broken Christians; the church I want to build will restore broken patterns." From day one as a church we've tried to build according to that mandate, to build restoration and renew people's trust in the Church in line with a New Testament pattern. The vision, which God so clearly laid on my heart when we founded the church, was, "Serving our community with a message of hope, truth and love." In many ways it was a statement of faith, a declaration of what we would become. It may have taken us ten years to get to this place, but I believe we are now beginning to walk in what we have declared. Now our focus is to fulfil the Isaiah 49 mandate that God gave us to get the salt out of the shaker and truly be "a light to the world".

> **" ... there are so many new and undiscovered ways to reach out and touch our community on all kinds of levels. Our job is to find them."**

What this means to us is that there are so many new and undiscovered ways to reach out and touch our community on all kinds of levels. Our job is to find them. One such expression is the work of one of our local primary school chaplains. Some time ago she visited our church to talk about some of the things happening in her school. She said,

> "I'm running a youth Alpha course at the moment. 25–30 kids have been coming along to it. Seven of those young people gave their hearts to Jesus last Friday, which was really exciting. God is doing some good things. We're also running some lunchtime programs for the kids, as well as some other initiatives to try and link the school with the churches in the community."

She mentioned how her work in the school was beginning to draw young, non-Christian people into the church:

> "A couple of boys who attended the Alpha Course decided to come to your conference and I was able to

talk to them about their experiences at the conference and explain some of the things about God that had been brought up ... I believe those boys will make a commitment to Christ – you can tell when God is really speaking to someone. I'm going to encourage them to come back and check out your church. My job is not to bring everyone to church, but to partner with you.

God is doing some amazing things in the lives of the kids in the school. One of the female students, who had become a Christian a little while ago, asked me to pray for her because she had glandular fever. So we prayed together and several days later she caught me in the school yard and told me that God had healed her."

This should all serve to remind us that God doesn't just come out on Sundays to touch people's lives – He is working every day of the week if we'll let Him! We're so grateful for people like our chaplains and youth workers who are prepared to get stuck in amongst the young people of our schools and see miracles like this happen as God touches their lives. Even greater than that will be the day when our young people themselves begin to "be" the church in their schools, taking hold of Monday church principles. Then we'll see incredible works spring up in every school in our region.

If this all seems too much, Monday church can begin for you on a much simpler level. It can begin with any individual pursuing God's calling on their life. A career could just be a career, but in the hands of a person with a revelation of Monday church a career can become a strategic position in the kingdom. God told my wife, Sharonne, to go to university and get a teaching degree. She pursued this so that she would be qualified to help those children in our community with learning difficulties – especially the cases no one else wanted to handle. When we begin to make this kind of life decision, it won't all be smooth sailing, but we should expect the favour of God. As Sharonne began working with the kids the Government gave her a grant to help with the set up costs of her Monday church initiative! She now tutors kids individually and helps each one according to their needs. Every family of every child is being exposed to the love of Jesus – a different Jesus than the one they thought they knew about – and a church that is relevant because it is seeking to meet their needs. I can assure you, the Government loves Monday church! They have blessed us with grants for things like a mobile soup kitchen – a trailer that can be taken out onto the streets so that we can begin to feed street kids and other homeless people – as well as other projects and initiatives of Monday church in the community.

God has called us to live a Christianity that is authentic and real out there, that touches people with the compassion of Christ. This is vital if the Church is not to dry up and become irrelevant. Many of us haven't engaged in community action because we've been trained to leave it to "the professionals", but we are not truly the Church unless we have a passion and compassion for the lost and hurting.

CHAPTER 5

OUR JOURNEY— YOUR JOURNEY?

It's easy in a book like this to give the impression that we just began focusing on the Monday church paradigm and every thing went fantastically well. Of course, the reality is quite different. God had to take us on a journey lasting several years, gently guiding and prodding us in the right direction so that we could begin to grasp how radically He wanted us to change in order to take the Gospel beyond our four walls and into the community.

The journey really began in 1994. At the time I was running a youth camp in a small country town when I felt God speak to me so clearly that He was about to reposition me. This was something of a scary prospect for a person who'd only ever been in two churches my whole life. Nervous and a little excited I kept the experience largely to myself and waited to see what God would do. I didn't have to wait very long when my senior pastor at the time came to me and said, "I need to send you to a little church on the south side of Adelaide. There's been some struggles and I just need you to go and love the people. It'll probably only be for about three months until I can find them a senior pastor." But inside me I knew that this was "it". God had given me Isaiah 49:9 as a mandate and over the following months had continued to stir my heart with vision and purpose. I knew it would be tough and I knew there would be struggles, but I also knew that there was such purpose behind it all.

Three years prior to this God had begun to birth in me a vision for the kind of church He wanted to build and I wanted to belong to. Isaiah 49 had become the passage of Scripture that defined so much about what that was. My own notes describing what I was seeing were scribbled at various points throughout my journal. For a while I treated these verses as specific to me, rather than for the church as a whole. After all, I wasn't a senior leader. But as the purpose of God began to unfold it became so clear to me that I had been shown a snapshot of what He was calling me to be a part of. Isaiah 49 became such a consistent theme with many of the key staff that God brought to us. Many new people who came to join us would say things like, "I'm not sure of the significance of this, but I believe God has spoken to me from Isaiah 49 . . . " It was obvious that God was up to something.

Isaiah 49:1–6 says this:

"Listen to me, all you in distant lands!
  Pay attention, you who are far away!
The LORD called me before my birth;
  from within the womb he called me by name.

> *He made my words of judgment as sharp as a sword.*
>   *He has hidden me in the shadow of his hand.*
>   *I am like a sharp arrow in his quiver.*
>
> *He said to me, 'You are my servant, Israel,*
>   *and you will bring me glory.'*
>
> *I replied, 'But my work seems so useless!*
>   *I have spent my strength for nothing and to no purpose.*
> *Yet I leave it all in the Lord's hand;*
>   *I will trust God for my reward."*
>
> *And now the LORD speaks —*
>   *the one who formed me in my mother's womb to be his servant,*
>   *who commissioned me to bring Israel back to him.*
> *The LORD has honoured me,*
>   *and my God has given me strength.*
> *He says, 'You will do more than restore the people of Israel to me.*
>   *I will make you a light to the Gentiles,*
>   *and you will bring my salvation to the ends of the earth.' "*

Later, Isaiah writes this:

> *"This is what the Sovereign LORD says:*
>   *'See, I will give a signal to the godless nations.*
> *They will carry your little sons back to you in their arms;*
>   *they will bring your daughters on their shoulders.*
> *Kings and queens will serve you ... ' "*
>
> (ISAIAH 49:22–23)

Isaiah 49:5 became a verse of particular significance to us. God said, " ... restore the people of Israel to me." That was the first part of His mandate for us as a church. We had such a burden and indeed a mandate to restore people who had, for whatever reason, turned their back on the Church. We had a function to perform in seeing disillusioned Christians restored to a vibrant faith in Christ. This was a great starting point.

Over the last ten years, one of the great things God has done through us is that He has given us a strategy and the influence to see many people "restored" by His love and truth. But people have not only been restored, but transformed too, given a renewed trust in the Church and more importantly have been reconnected with God. It has happened through the consistency of our message which in no small part is due to God's grace on our church. Ten years ago it was very hard to earn the right to be heard by Christians, many of whom thought we were too good to be true. Most were sceptical about me, the church we were trying to build, and the vision we were setting out to achieve. In fact, the typical reaction was, "It's all good for them now, but just wait till the honeymoon is over and reality sets in." But over time people discovered that we were for real and many of them began a journey of restoration and renewal in their passion for God and His kingdom.

When God speaks to you prophetically that word grows and expands over time. Usually we only grasp the full implications of what God has spoken to us after we have lived with the word for several years. Over time God will show us the bigger picture concerning His purposes, revealing it little by little so we can handle it. In the same way, over time, God "upgraded" His word to us and began to speak to us further from Isaiah 49 verse 6 which says,

> *"You will do **more than** restore the people of Israel to me.*
> *I will make you a light to the Gentiles . . . "*

(emphasis added)

It became apparent to me that the first ten years for our church were about a restoration of biblical truth, which would bring about the restoration of many people's lives. During that time God burdened our hearts for the restoration of biblical governance with apostolic leadership and prophetic confirmation, mutual accountability and increasing openness. We saw a "revival structure" come into place which created room for God to move. We certainly haven't arrived yet, of course, but God in His grace has given us a model prophetically which has not only brought growth and life to our church, but that others have been able to copy and find success with. As a church we are intent on building a family according to a biblical pattern because we want to see God's kingdom come.

As God expanded this verse for us we saw that the subsequent years would be about reaching out to those beyond the church, reaching "more than" just believers and bringing them to Christ. God launched us on a mission to serve our community with a message of "hope, truth and love". If all we did was bless and restore Christians then we would be like salt that is still stuck in its shaker. Now it was time for us to get the salt out and spread it further. It was time to be a "light to the Gentiles" – the communities all around us.

That was the point at which God began to speak to us about renovating schools, hospitals and prisons. Why renovation? I believe it's a spiritual principle: the natural so often prophesies to and precedes the spiritual. As we began a natural renovation of buildings, resulting in a positive effect on people's lives, so we saw a renovation in the Spirit as the practical love of Christ touched people and changed them.

At the same time, God began speaking to us about reaching out to the nations, about taking successful biblical patterns and refreshing and revitalising churches all over the world through what God had done in us. We have a mandate to disciple and build significant leaders throughout the world, not only through instruction, but also through relationship and connection. I recently spoke to a young man from our city

85

campus who told me he wanted to return to his native Malaysia and start a revival there. "I want this church to train me before I go back," he said. It has become so clear to us that we now need to initiate a global vision that will reach out to a diverse spectrum of people. God's word to us was so clear: "Don't stop restoring people who are Christians; don't stop building biblical structures; but reach out to not yet Christians and be committed to world missions."

THE SPIRIT OF ELIJAH

I believe that the journey we have embarked on as a church is not uniquely marked out for us. It's not simply "our journey", I believe what we have seen is a microcosm of God's heart for His universal Church. Our journey could be your journey too. He wants all of His people everywhere to stand up boldly and go against the flow, confronting the spirit of the age by demonstrating the love of Christ in a loveless society. I believe that, prophetically, the spirit of Elijah is coming upon God's Church once again to embolden God's people to engage with society and the State in a way that we haven't done for many years. This is why Monday church is being birthed in many different places by many different people, and why more people must grasp the vision and run with it.

Secularism and immorality has characterised Western society for a long time, but God is raising up His Church to initiate change. God has given me a vision of seeing men and women of God who will stand against the spirit of this age. Against a tide of immorality that wants to give licence to sin, the Church will rise with not only grace and love but the Spirit of truth and power.

I have the privilege of travelling quite a bit and in a number of recent meetings I've attended, speaker after speaker has stood up and spoken about the coming of the spirit of Elijah on the earth. In fact, at one conference I attended every single speaker spoke about it, and none of them had compared notes or knew in advance what the others were going to say. I think that when God repeats Himself like that He's really trying to get our attention.

> "...the journey we have embarked on as a church is not uniquely marked out for us. It's not simply 'our journey', I believe what we have seen is a microcosm of God's heart for His universal Church."

Recently, I re-read the verses in Acts 4:5–13 about Peter and John healing a crippled man and being hauled before the religious authorities because of it:

"The next day the council of all the rulers and elders and teachers of religious law met in Jerusalem. Annas the high priest was there, along with Caiaphas, John, Alexander, and other relatives of the high priest. They brought in the two disciples and demanded, 'By what power, or in whose name, have you done this?'"

(verses 5–7)

A phrase in the following verse stood out to me: *"Then Peter, filled with the Holy Spirit, said to them, 'Rulers and elders of our people...'"*

The political leaders and the religious leaders of Peter and John's day were the *same* people. There was no division between religion and State. So Peter was addressing the political leaders of the nation when he said,

"Rulers and elders of our people, are we being questioned today because we've done a good deed for a crippled man? Do you want to

know how he was healed? Let me clearly state to all of you and to all the people of Israel that he was healed by the powerful name of Jesus Christ the Nazarene, **the man you crucified** *..."*

(verses 8–10, emphasis added)

What incredible boldness! And he goes on to say:

"... but whom God raised from the dead. For Jesus is the one referred to in the Scriptures, where it says,

> *'The stone that you builders rejected*
> *has now become the cornerstone.'*

There is salvation in no one else! God has given no other name under heaven by which we must be saved."

(verses 10–12)

The reaction of the Council to this speech is amazing:

"The members of the council were **amazed** *when they saw the* **boldness** *of Peter and John, for they could see that they were* **ordinary men with no special training** *in the Scriptures. They also recognized them* **as men who had been with Jesus.***"*

(verse 13, emphasis added)

We are beginning to see the Church bring to bear a similar influence on our politicians. Recently, a politician from our city visited me. He sat in my office and said, "I have visited your church on several occasions and when I first started coming I knew *about* Jesus. I've now fallen in love with Him and I *know* Him. Will you pray for me today that I will never deny my faith in the courts of government, because I would rather lose my position as a politician than deny the Lord Jesus Christ as my Lord and Saviour?"

What a humbling situation. "Who am I, Lord," I thought,

"that I should have the privilege of praying for a key politician?" But this is how it works in God's kingdom. Peter and John were ordinary, uneducated men, yet they had a boldness (not an arrogance) that came from Heaven. We, the contemporary Church, need to have that same boldness, a boldness that wants to see future generations blessed, so we will rise up and fight for our children and grandchildren to see them touched by God. We will minister to a nation that desperately needs Jesus. I can't say that I feel educated enough or prepared enough to do that, but with a passion I want our communities to look at us and conclude, "Those people have been with Jesus. There is no other explanation."

Malachi 4:5–6 tells us specifically what the purpose of the spirit of Elijah will be:

> *"Look, I am sending you the prophet Elijah before the great and dreadful day of the LORD arrives. His preaching will turn the hearts of fathers to their children, and the hearts of children to their fathers. Otherwise I will come and strike the land with a curse."*
>
> (Malachi 4:5–6)

The Bible teaches us that in the last days the anointing of Elijah is coming upon God's people to bring about reconciliation. The result will be that the "fathers'" hearts will be joined back with their "sons" and the sons' back to their fathers. In other words, we will see generational blessing and reconciliation take place in the kingdom of God. Our church has been so blessed in the expression of love between the generations as we have embraced the idea that our God is a "generational God", not a "next generation" or a "previous generation" God.

If we want to increasingly see these things happening in our churches then we have got to develop a new culture of prayer. You cannot change a nation without prayer! Peter and John knew what it meant to seek God's face in prayer daily. If we want to see a crippled generation healed then we must do the same. We have to be dependent upon God. How do we confront the spirit of the age? By prayer and proclamation, by connecting with our communities, by being a blessing and bringing the full truth of God's Word to bear. This can be your church's journey.

PART THREE

CHANGING YOUR CHURCH CULTURE

CHAPTER 6

COME LET US REASON TOGETHER

Growing up in church most of my life, the words of Isaiah 1:18 were not new to me:

> " 'Come now, let's settle this,'
>   says the LORD.
> 'Though your sins are like scarlet,
>   I will make them as white as snow.
> Though they are red like crimson,
>   I will make them as white as wool.' "

93

I couldn't count the times that I have heard this scripture used at the end of a service to invite people to come to Christ. While that is in keeping with the tenor of God's Word it is important to know that in its original context this verse has nothing to do with people coming to personal faith. The context of this passage of Scripture is God speaking to a nation that is living in disobedience because of their indifference to the poor, needy and broken all around them. Earlier, in verse 10, God has chastised them saying,

> *"Listen to the LORD, you leaders of 'Sodom.'*
>   *Listen to the law of our God, people of 'Gomorrah.'"*

The Contemporary English Version of the Bible makes it even clearer: *"You are no better than the leaders and people of Sodom and Gomorrah!"*

Ezekiel 16:49 gives us the description of what the sins of Sodom were:

> *"Sodom's sins were pride, gluttony, and laziness, while the poor and needy suffered outside her door."*

Because of all this sin and disobedience God said to His people, *"Come . . . "* and offered them forgiveness if they would turn to Him and repent. As I read this scripture afresh recently, that first word alone impacted me deeply: "Come!" The God of the universe speaks to us in our sin, disobedience and unrighteousness and asks us to come! Not only that but He says, *"Come **now** . . . "* He gives us an opportunity *today* to respond to Him. Then God says, *"Let's settle this . . . "* In other words, He says to us, "Come here, let's discuss this problem and see if we can resolve it." God doesn't say, "Come here now and let me tell you off!" because He wants a relationship with us. He wants to interact with us, to get us to hear and understand His heart towards us personally and mankind in general. He wants to communicate!

Given the people's disobedience God could easily have said "Go" instead of "Come". He could have said, "Go! Get out of my presence." When my kids were growing up, if they were continually naughty, we would get to a stage where we would say, "Go! I'm sick of telling you this over and over again. I'll talk to you later because I'm too angry now!" God could have done that and been perfectly justified, but the patience and love of God towards His people caused Him to say, *"Come now, let us reason together"* (NIV).

Isaiah 1:18 can be summarised as follows:

- *"Come"* – it's about hearing God.
- *"Now"* – it's about timing and the time is now!
- *"Let us"* – not "let Me", God wants to work in relationship.
- *"Reason together"* – it's about receiving the revelation God has for His Church.
- *"and your sins … white as snow"* – the change is like the difference between red and white.

I believe there is a discourse going on right now between God and His Church and the Lord is saying to us, "Come now, let's reason together. Let's discuss this because there is something I really want you to understand…" A tension has arisen in the Church – a struggle between our religious ways and traditions and what the Spirit of God wants to do in and among us. God is constantly on the move, doing new things, and we in our humanity easily get stuck in a rut. Some of us are still doing things that were part of a move of God twenty years ago while God has moved on. We keep on doing them just because they are familiar and comfortable! What was once a movement for change has become a monument to tradition.

The message of this book could be seen as a threat to many happy, well-established churches because it calls for radical change. Please understand my heart. My intent is not to be controversial, nor to have change for change's sake. But, with all my heart I believe that if we will embrace the Monday church paradigm we will see revival break out in our nations. For that reason it is a message that is burning with an urgency inside of me. I have seen glimpses of the fruit and I know there is so much more. I am passionate about God's Church and so desire for it to be what it was designed to be!

> "...we all want to see a Church of power and influence, so I guess it comes down to how much we're willing to pay for it. Would we be willing to put aside our comfort and our preferences just to see what God might do?"

If you are one of those reading this saying, "I want to change, but it feels like an impossible, uphill struggle", take heart! God is the Master of transformation. In Isaiah 1:18 He is saying to His people, "No matter how deep the stain of your sins are, I can remove them and I can make you as clean as freshly fallen snow." No matter how red something is, God can make it white. In the same way He says to us, no matter how long your church has done things this way, I can turn it around for you if you are willing to reason it out with Me.

The challenge for the Church is that many of us are comfortable and have seen a measure of success and the necessity for change is not apparent. We can quite happily continue to maintain the status quo without causing any major discomfort. So why would we change? But I believe there is not a genuine Christian person who doesn't dream about the Church returning to its former greatness. I believe we all want to see a Church of power and influence, so I guess it comes down to how much we're willing to pay for it. Would we be willing to put aside our comfort and our preferences just to see what God might do?

When God began to speak to me about what was on His heart through Isaiah chapter 1 I was invited to go and speak to a forum being held in Tasmania. There were a number of other speakers there and the forum was made up of politicians, federal members of the Australian Parliament, and some community and church leaders.

Naturally I spoke on Isaiah chapter 1 and the things God was laying on my heart. As I did, I could see one of the other speakers nodding his head in agreement. After I had spoken, another speaker opened his Bible and continued to speak from Isaiah 1. You could call that a coincidence, but I think it was more of a God-incidence and now I was really listening to see what others would say.

When the third person got up to speak, he didn't speak from Isaiah 1, but his message was along very similar lines and at that moment I sensed the Holy Spirit speaking to me and the thought exploded in my head: "Danny, it's time to build two churches, two expressions of My Church." At the time I thought, "What does that mean?" But as the day went on the meaning became clear and I scribbled the following notes in my journal:

> "It's time to build Sunday church and Monday church. If we only build Sunday church the Church will become irrelevant in its community and society. If we only build Monday church we will become a social institution and become disconnected from our source."

As I wrote this, the revelation began to flow of what God was saying, what God is calling the Church to do and to be right now. The Holy Spirit showed me a picture of the difference between these two churches, how they are built and who builds them. My prayer is that as you read this it would come alive to you too and you would get hold of the revelation and realize the potential for transforming your own community.

WHAT KIND OF CHURCH DO WE NEED TO BECOME?

As we began to build Sunday-Monday church God gave me a picture of our church and what it could look like in ten years time if we obeyed Him. He showed me the following verses from Jeremiah 29, written to a people in captivity in Babylon:

> *"This is what the LORD of Heaven's Armies, the God of Israel, says to all the captives he has exiled to Babylon from Jerusalem: 'Build homes, and plan to stay. Plant gardens, and eat the food they produce. Marry and have children. Then find spouses for them so that you may have many grandchildren. Multiply! Do not dwindle away! And work for the peace and prosperity of the city where I sent you into exile. Pray to the LORD for it, for its welfare will determine your welfare.' This is what the LORD of Heaven's Armies, the God of Israel, says: 'Do not let your prophets and fortune-tellers who are with you in the land of Babylon trick you. Do not listen to their dreams, because they are telling you lies in my name. I have not sent them,' says the LORD."*
>
> (JEREMIAH 29:4–9)

Then continuing in verse 11:

> *"'For I know the plans I have for you,' says the LORD. 'They are plans for good and not for disaster, to give you a future and a hope. In those days when you pray, I will listen.'"*

I believe these verses don't just apply to individuals but to the Church corporately. They are the heart of God for His Church wherever it is expressed in a local body of believers. Unpacking these verses I see a church that is:

1. A real life church

God wants us to be successful in everyday life so that it becomes a witness to others. In the simple acts of life – building great families, building homes – God wants His Church to "do life" well. It means having a spirit of excellence and doing well in business as we put the concerns of God's kingdom first and foremost. This is not hype or prosperity teaching. Realistically, how can we give to the poor if we have a poverty mentality ourselves? We must learn to be good stewards of all that God has entrusted to us.

I want to see believers being blessed. I want your business to be blessed, your marriage to be blessed, I even want your garden to be blessed so that you win a prize for having the best roses in your street! Why? Because if you do life well it tells everyone around you something about who you represent. If you never mow your lawn and the gutters are hanging off your house and you tell someone you love Jesus, they might well think to themselves, "Yeah, that's a Jesus I can do without!" But being faithful in life, stable in our jobs, having successful families and prospering through good stewardship – that's a real life church that will make people sit up and take notice.

2. A relationship church

We also need to be a church that thrives on relationships, a church that embraces all generations. I love it when I see families in church where there are grandparents, parents and children, all from the same family, and when you see different families connecting through marriage. We need to be a generational church too. Recently a young couple got married in our church and I felt so proud of them because I felt like one of their dads, even though technically I'm not one of their dads! These are "our" kids in our church.

3. A church that reaches the community
Enough said. If you look after Babylon then you will have peace!

4. A church that relies on God through prayer
The last thing these verses teach us is that we are nothing if we are not reliant on God in prayer. It is His grace upon our lives that will cause our good works to impact and transform our communities.

To summarise, we can think of these attributes as 4 Rs:

1. A real life church
2. A relationship church
3. A reaching out church
4. A relying-on-God church

If we concentrate on being these four things then we will be like a sweet-smelling fragrance to our community and people will look at us and say, "We want whatever it is they have." That is my prayer.

CHANGING THE ATMOSPHERE OF YOUR CHURCH

As the understanding of what God has said to me about building Sunday-Monday church has grown it has become clear to me that we need to base the church on certain non-negotiable values. God spoke clearly to us about this and gave us eight distinct areas to focus on. I call them the Eight

Atmospheres and they have become an integral part of our DNA and our teaching. I share them here because I believe they are valuable "tests" for any church leader to use. You can apply them to your own church as a guide to see how you are doing in each area.

A Godly Atmosphere

To me this speaks of the fact that we must have integrity in everything we do and this must follow through in every area of church life and leadership. We cannot have what someone has described as "selective integrity", where we uphold the truth in some areas of our life but not in others. This means being open about everything to do with church life. Our church's financial accounts, for instance, are freely available to anyone – and every other area of church life is open to scrutiny as well. People should be able to come and inspect what happens in the life of the church at any time and find out what is going on.

It also means having due respect for the authority of God's Word. The Bible doesn't just contain the *words* of God, it is the *Word* of God. Therefore we must live according to God's Word and our morality must fall into line with it, rather than following what society says about how we should live. So much of the Church around the world is limiting God by diluting the power of His Word. Affirmation of the power of the Word will help to build a godly atmosphere.

A Grace Atmosphere

God loves us and accepts us for who we are, but because He loves us He is not content to leave us that way. His plan is for us to be completely transformed over time by His grace. A grace-filled church is one that doesn't get caught up with rules and regulations, but is committed to the love of God progressively changing people's lives as they become more like Jesus.

I love the song, "Jesus, You're My Friend". What a deep truth. We have become friends with Christ and friends with God through Him. The God of the universe is our friend! So many people abuse the name of Jesus and use it as a swear word, but how good it is to find a church that honours His name and whose atmosphere is full of grace, welcoming everyone who visits and helping them to find God as their friend.

A Gathering Atmosphere

A gathering atmosphere describes a church that has a desire to unify rather than divide; a church that brings people and lives together, one that has a strong sense of "family". It is important to have a church that "gathers" people. But not only people. We believe we're called to gather and provide "resources", not just financial, but in providing teaching, training and people resources, that we might leave an inheritance for the generations.

> **"Growth that happens within a church purely because of the birth rate of its families and by the transfer growth of Christians moving from other churches is not healthy growth. The bulk of the people who will be members of our church in the future should not yet even be believers!"**

A Growing Atmosphere

The issue of growth is not just the issue of evangelism. Someone once said, "All healthy things grow" and this applies to churches too. We must be concerned with getting the salt out of the shaker to do its work. Growth that happens within a church purely because of the birth rate of its families and by the transfer growth of Christians moving from other churches is not healthy growth. The bulk of the people who will be members of our church in the future should not yet even be believers! We must also have a passion to build "bigger" people. If you want a bigger, more influential church then build bigger, more influential people. Good quality discipleship and training are an essential part of a growing atmosphere.

A Generations Atmosphere

I love the young people of our church and what I love most about them is that they love the senior members of our congregation. There doesn't appear to be much of a generation gap. My philosophy is that there will always be genera-tional "perceptions" but there should never be a "gap". We want an atmosphere of partnership amongst the generations, each acknowledging the strengths of the other and partnering together to see our world changed to build something sig-nificant for Jesus. The emerging generation need the love, acceptance and wisdom of the older generation, while the older generation need the life, enthusiasm and innovation of the younger generation. We need to build churches that recognise, understand and embrace these differences.

A Generous Atmosphere

We aim to be a generous church and I don't just mean financially. We seek to be generous with our time and generous in helping other churches. From Monday to Sunday we are constantly reaching out to our community and seeking to commit acts of unwarranted generosity.

A Guiding Atmosphere

We recognise the fact that people come to the church to get well, emotionally, mentally and spiritually. The Church should be a place for sick people to get well! So we aim to spend time helping people to come to wholeness and we do this through training and discipleship, equipping people to live their lives directed and motivated by purpose, and by giving them the skills to be successful in life as much as we can. But life can be very difficult at times and sometimes we need a little extra direction in those difficult seasons. We do our best to provide help through godly, biblically-based counselling.

A Great Atmosphere

I believe in having the spirit of excellence running through everything we do. This is not to show off or say, "Haven't we got a brilliant church?" We just want to demonstrate to God that we are doing everything we can to the very best of our ability for His glory. A great atmosphere is created wherever excellence flows. Excellence has very little to do with the size of your church or your budget, it's simply doing the very best with whatever you have in your hand. When we do that in every area of church life it says to God and to others that we are serious about honouring Him.

Doing Sunday-Monday church is no longer a project for us, it's our passion! And we can see so clearly that it is God's mandate for His whole Church. Even as I complete this book another hospital renovation has taken place, mobilizing 377 volunteers from the Christian churches of Adelaide to renovate the out-patient area of the Women's and Children's Hospital, impacting the lives of the approximately 300,000 people who walk through its doors every year. Our community has been blessed and the Church made visible once again.

We have also had the great privilege of renovating a church on the other side of our city desperately in need of upgrade and refurbishment – Monday church blessing somebody else's

Sunday church, giving the brand new pastors a great head start to build something significant in our city, something beyond just a local church, hopefully inspiring it to become a community-focused "salt out of the shaker" church. The most amazing thing to see was the not-yet-Christians from the local community partnering with us.

It's a new day. I know where God goes on Monday! Let's declare together the words of Jesus from the Gospel of John:

> *"All of us must quickly carry out the tasks assigned us by the one who sent me because there is little time left before the night falls and all the work comes to an end. But while I'm still here in the world I am the light of the world."*

(JOHN 9:4)

So I guess the question is, what's your vision? What will you do about Monday church? It's time to see it, it's time to speak it and, most importantly, it's time to start. Bless you as you build.

ABOUT THE AUTHOR

Danny Guglielmucci and his wife Sharonne are the Senior Ministers of Edge Church International, a dynamic multi-site church based in Adelaide, South Australia. Danny's strong apostolic leadership, coupled with his genuine pastor's heart, has been instrumental in seeing this vibrant church grow from just 30 people in 1994, to over 5,000 meeting across three locations in Adelaide. He also oversees Edge Church's most recent church plant in Bristol, England.

Danny is renowned for his passion for people and his desire to see leaders grow in God. His pastoral oversight extends from individuals in the church, to pastors on the other side of the world. Danny is a much sought after communicator, sharing life-changing truths in a practical, down to earth manner.

He travels extensively around the world, preaching and teaching at churches, leadership summits, retreats and National and State conferences. His leadership teaching and life message assist local churches in building according to God's pattern.

Danny established and oversees Edge Connect events, which are designed to encourage and equip pastors and leaders both nationally and internationally. He also provides leadership to other churches as a member of the National Executive of Australian Christian Churches (previously the Assemblies of God in Australia).

Danny's wife Sharonne is a qualified school teacher who works in helping children with learning difficulties in a revolutionary extra-curricular program. Danny and Sharonne have three children, Kris, Michael and Danielle.

CONTACT
INFORMATION

Edge Church International
Phone: +61 8 8322 2888
Fax: +61 8 8322 8101
Postal address: PO Box 106, Reynella, SA, Australia 5161
Website: www.edgechurch.com

We hope you enjoyed reading this New Wine book.
For details of other New Wine books
and a range of 2,000 titles from other
Word and Spirit publishers visit our website:
www.newwineministries.co.uk
email: newwine@xalt.co.uk